Progress on Transboundary Water Cooperation

Global baseline for SDG indicator 6.5.2

—————

2018

Presenting the UN-Water Integrated Monitoring Initiative for SDG 6

Through the UN-Water Integrated Monitoring Initiative for Sustainable Development Goal (SDG) 6, the United Nations seeks to support countries in monitoring water- and sanitation-related issues within the framework of the 2030 Agenda for Sustainable Development, and in compiling country data to report on global progress towards SDG 6.

The Initiative brings together the United Nations organizations that are formally mandated to compile country data on the SDG 6 global indicators, who organize their work within three complementary initiatives:

- **WHO/UNICEF Joint Monitoring Programme for Water Supply, Sanitation and Hygiene (JMP)**[1]

  Building on its 15 years of experience from Millennium Development Goals (MDG) monitoring, the JMP looks after the drinking water, sanitation and hygiene aspects of SDG 6 (targets 6.1 and 6.2).

- **Integrated Monitoring of Water and Sanitation-Related SDG Targets (GEMI)**[2]

  GEMI was established in 2014 to harmonize and expand existing monitoring efforts focused on water, wastewater and ecosystem resources (targets 6.3 to 6.6).

- **UN-Water Global Analysis and Assessment of Sanitation and Drinking-Water (GLAAS)**[3]

  The means of implementing SDG 6 (targets 6.a and 6.b) fall under the remit of GLAAS, which monitors the inputs and the enabling environment required to sustain and develop water and sanitation systems and services.

The objectives of the Integrated Monitoring Initiative are to:

- Develop methodologies and tools to monitor SDG 6 global indicators

- Raise awareness at the national and global levels about SDG 6 monitoring

- Enhance technical and institutional country capacity for monitoring

- Compile country data and report on global progress towards SDG 6

The joint effort around SDG 6 is especially important in terms of the institutional aspects of monitoring, including the integration of data collection and analysis across sectors, regions and administrative levels.

To learn more about water and sanitation in the 2030 Agenda for Sustainable Development, and the Integrated Monitoring Initiative for SDG 6, visit our website: www.sdg6monitoring.org

INDICATORS	CUSTODIANS
6.1.1 Proportion of population using safely managed drinking water services	WHO, UNICEF
6.2.1 Proportion of population using safely managed sanitation services, including a hand-washing facility with soap and water	WHO, UNICEF
6.3.1 Proportion of wastewater safely treated	WHO, UN-Habitat, UNSD
6.3.2 Proportion of bodies of water with good ambient water quality	UN Environment
6.4.1 Change in water-use efficiency over time	FAO
6.4.2 Level of water stress: freshwater withdrawal as a proportion of available freshwater resources	FAO
6.5.1 Degree of integrated water resources management implementation (0-100)	UN Environment
6.5.2 Proportion of transboundary basin area with an operational arrangement for water cooperation	UNESCO, UNECE
6.6.1 Change in the extent of water-related ecosystems over time	UN Environment, Ramsar
6.a.1 Amount of water- and sanitation-related official development assistance that is part of a government-coordinated spending plan	WHO, UN Environment, OECD
6.b.1 Proportion of local administrative units with established and operational policies and procedures for participation of local communities in water and sanitation management	WHO, UN Environment, OECD

[1] http://www.sdg6monitoring.org/about/components/jmp/
[2] http://www.sdg6monitoring.org/about/components/presenting-gemi/
[3] http://www.sdg6monitoring.org/about/components/glaas/

CONTENTS

Nile River seen from space. Photo: Stuart Rankin/Creative Commons

FOREWORD

Water is the lifeblood of ecosystems, vital to human health and well-being and a precondition for economic prosperity. That is why it is at the very core of the 2030 Agenda for Sustainable Development. Sustainable Development Goal 6 (SDG 6), the availability and sustainable management of water and sanitation for all, has strong links to all of the other SDGs.

In this series of progress reports under the UN-Water Integrated Monitoring Initiative for SDG 6, we evaluate progress towards this vital goal. The United Nations organizations are working together to help countries monitor water and sanitation across sectors and compile data so that we can report on global progress.

SDG 6 expands the Millennium Development Goal focus on drinking water and basic sanitation to include the management of water and wastewater and ecosystems, across boundaries of all kinds. Bringing these aspects together is an essential first step towards breaking down sector fragmentation and enabling coherent and sustainable management, and hence towards a future where water use is sustainable.

This report is part of a series that track progress towards the various targets set out in SDG 6 using the SDG global indicators. The reports are based on country data, compiled and verified by the responsible United Nations organizations, and sometimes complemented by data from other sources. The main beneficiaries of better data are countries. The 2030 Agenda specifies that global follow-up and review "will be primarily based on national official data sources", so we sorely need stronger national statistical systems. This will involve developing technical and institutional capacity and infrastructure for more effective monitoring.

To review overall progress towards SDG 6 and identify interlinkages and ways to accelerate progress, UN-Water produced the SDG 6 Synthesis Report 2018 on Water and Sanitation. It concluded that the world is not on track to achieve SDG 6 by 2030. This finding was discussed by Member States during the High-level Political Forum on Sustainable Development (HLPF) in July 2018. Delegates sounded the alarm about declining official development aid to the water sector and stressed the need for finance, high-level political support, leadership and enhanced collaboration within and across countries if SDG 6 and its targets are to be met.

To achieve SDG 6, we need to monitor and report progress. This will help decision makers identify and prioritize what, when and where interventions are needed to improve implementation. Information on progress is also essential to ensure accountability and generate political, public and private sector support for investment. The UN-Water Integrated Monitoring Initiative for SDG 6 is an essential element of the United Nations' determination to ensure the availability and sustainable management of water and sanitation for all by 2030.

Gilbert F. Houngbo
UN-Water Chair and President of the International
Fund for Agricultural Development

FOREWORD

When the Heads of State, government leaders and high-level representatives of the United Nations and civil society came together at the seventieth session of the General Assembly in September 2015, they adopted an ambitious Agenda designed to ensure prosperity for all while protecting our planet and strengthening the foundations for peace.

This 2030 Agenda for Sustainable Development seeks to transform society and put it on the path towards sustainable development for all. The 17 Sustainable Development Goals and their framework of targets and indicators play an important role in that process by embodying the international community's commitment not only to the Goals, but to accountability in their efforts to achieve them.

This commitment is evident in Sustainable Development Goal indicator 6.5.2, that is the focus of this report. Through Sustainable Development Goal indicator 6.5.2, efforts to put in place operational arrangements for transboundary water cooperation can now be monitored. Monitoring and further strengthening transboundary water cooperation are central to ensuring sustainable development for all. A total of 153 countries worldwide share transboundary river and lake basins and aquifer systems which, together, cover over half of the Earth's land surface, account for an estimated 60 per cent of global freshwater flow and are home to more than 40 per cent of the world's population.

While there are still challenges to the collection and analysis of data, the outcome of the first indicator 6.5.2 monitoring exercise, presented in this report, is proof of the need for a significant effort to ensure that operational arrangements for all transboundary rivers, lakes and aquifers are in place by 2030. Although this finding is sobering, the fact that the report exists is, in itself, a significant milestone in our ambition to improve transboundary water cooperation. It is particularly encouraging that during the first reporting exercise, 107 of the 153 countries that share transboundary waters provided data on the status of their transboundary water cooperation. This high response rate demonstrates the international community's commitment to monitoring the Sustainable Development Goals and bodes well for further monitoring of indicator 6.5.2.

As co-custodians for indicator 6.5.2, the United Nations Economic Commission for Europe (ECE) and the United Nations Educational, Scientific and Cultural Organization (UNESCO) are strongly committed to supporting the monitoring exercise. In addition, through activities such as those of the Convention on the Protection and Use of Transboundary Watercourses and International Lakes, serviced by the ECE, and those of the UNESCO International Hydrological Programme, both ECE and UNESCO directly support transboundary water cooperation as a catalyst for sustainable development. The monitoring of indicator 6.5.2 and the findings contained in this report can give much-needed impetus to transboundary water cooperation around the world.

Olga Algayerova
Executive Secretary
of the United Nations
Economic Commission
for Europe

Flavia Schlegel
Assistant Director
General for Natural Sciences,
United Nations Educational,
Cultural and Scientific
Organization

ACKNOWLEDGEMENTS

This publication was prepared by the United Nations Economic Commission for Europe (UNECE) and the United Nations Educational, Scientific and Cultural Organization (UNESCO) in their capacity as co-custodian agencies of Sustainable Development Goal (SDG) indicator 6.5.2, and on behalf of UN-Water. The list of UN-Water members and partners can be found on the following website – www.unwater.org. UNECE and UNESCO express their gratitude to the Governments that participated in the first SDG indicator 6.5.2 reporting exercise.

The drafting and editorial group was composed of:
– UNECE: Alistair Rieu-Clarke (lead), Francesca Bernardini, Sarah Tiefenauer-Linardon;
– UNESCO: Gabin Archambault, Alice Aureli, Aurélien Dumont, Jac van der Gun, Johannes C. Nonner, Marcello Serrao

This publication would not have been possible without funding from the Governments of Austria, Italy, Germany, the Netherlands, Sweden and Switzerland.

KEY MESSAGES

Transboundary water cooperation is critical for ensuring sustainable management of water resources and achieving Sustainable Development Goal (SDG) 6. Across the world, 153 countries share rivers, lakes and aquifers. Transboundary basins cover more than half of the Earth's land surface, account for an estimated 60 per cent of global freshwater flow and are home to more than 40 per cent of the world's population.

Transboundary water cooperation is a precondition for sustainable development, peace and stability. Transboundary waters create social, economic, environmental and political inter-dependencies. They not only sustain populations across borders but also connect economic sectors and ecosystems in the basins. Conflicting demands over shared waters can engender political conflicts and regional instability.

As the only target in the 2030 Agenda for Sustainable Development explicitly referring to transboundary cooperation, target 6.5 can play a catalytic role across multiple SDGs and targets. It can generate multiple benefits relating to the protection of human health, renewable energy provision, sustainable agriculture, climate adaptation, ecosystem protection, and peace and security.

Cooperation is shaped by the particular historical, legal and political context, and existing arrangements vary considerably in terms of scope and intensity of cooperation. They all reflect a tangible commitment by the countries involved to manage water resources at the transboundary level and are founded upon customary international law principles. Basin-specific arrangements are greatly supported by regional and global frameworks such as the Water Convention, the Watercourses Convention, the European Commission (EU) Water Framework Directive and the Revised Southern Africa Development Community (SADC) Protocol.

In some regions and basins, significant progress has been made to further transboundary water cooperation through operational arrangements. Progress is particularly advanced in Europe and Northern America, and in most major river and lake basins in sub-Saharan Africa. Regional legal frameworks, such as the EU Water Framework Directive and the Revised SADC Protocol, have proven to be important drivers of transboundary water cooperation.

However, results from the 6.5.2 indicator monitoring exercises show that arrangements for transboundary water cooperation are often absent. The first SDG indicator 6.5.2 monitoring exercise has demonstrated that for the 62 countries considered in this first assessment, only 59 per cent of their transboundary basin area is covered by operational arrangements, while only 17 countries have all their transboundary basins covered by operational arrangements. These results are consistent with those for SDG indicator 6.5.1.

Cooperation on transboundary aquifers represents a particular challenge and is lagging further behind. Despite the numerous services that groundwater provides for both humans and ecosystems, operational arrangements for transboundary aquifers are still rare around the world. Transboundary aquifers entered late on the scientific and political agendas, probably to a large extent on account of the hidden nature of groundwater. Delineating transboundary aquifers and realizing commitments to coordinated or joint management of this invisible resource therefore pose particular challenges.

If target 6.5 is to be achieved by 2030, progress must be accelerated and all transboundary basins must be covered by an operational arrangement. At the current rate of progress, with on average three agreements entered into per year, we are not on track to achieve target 6.5.

To this end, we need to capitalize on the experience and outputs of the first SDG indicator 6.5.2 reporting exercise. For the first time, a country-based process provides a robust methodology for monitoring cooperation on the world's transboundary basins. This can play an important role in advancing transboundary cooperation. It is important that countries and regions where reporting levels are currently low also engage in reporting exercises, and that synergies between reporting on 6.5.1 and 6.5.2 are exploited. Moreover, SDG indicator 6.5.2 reports should be used to set national and basin-specific targets related to transboundary water cooperation.

Cooperation can be strengthened by capitalizing on the momentum in support of the Convention on the Law of the Non-navigational Uses of International Watercourses (Watercourses Convention), the Convention on the Protection and Use of Transboundary Watercourses and International Lakes (Water Convention) and the Draft Articles on the Law of Transboundary Aquifers, sharing knowledge and experience of the benefits of transboundary water cooperation, improving financing for transboundary water cooperation and increasing capacity-building initiatives.

1

Introduction and background

1.1. Transboundary water cooperation and integrated water resources management

Through the adoption of 17 Sustainable Development Goals (SDGs) and 169 targets, the 2030 Agenda for Sustainable Development sets forth a "supremely ambitious and transformational vision" for people, planet and prosperity.[1] This level of ambition is reflected in SDG target 6.5, which seeks to implement integrated water resources management (IWRM) at all levels, including through transboundary cooperation as appropriate. IWRM calls for "the coordinated development and management of water, land and related resources, in order to maximize the resultant economic and social welfare in an equitable manner without compromising the sustainability of vital ecosystems".[2] With its focus on coordinated development and management, SDG target 6.5 lies at the heart of the SDG framework, offering an important means by which to reconcile competing needs and interests and advance a multitude of SDGs and their targets in an equitable and sustainable manner.[3]

From a transboundary water perspective, while SDG target 6.5 builds upon previous initiatives – such as the Mar del Plata Action Plan, Agenda 21 and the Rio+20 Plan of Implementation – its explicit recognition of the need for cooperation at the transboundary level is a significant step forward.[4] Further emphasis on transboundary water cooperation is embodied in SDG indicator 6.5.2, which seeks to measure the proportion of transboundary basin area with an operational arrangement for cooperation. SDG indicator 6.5.2 offers a complement to SDG indicator 6.5.1, which tracks the degree of IWRM implementation at all levels, including transboundary, by assessing four components of IWRM: enabling environment; institutions and participation; management instruments and financing.[5]

KEY FACTS

Transboundary water cooperation is critical to achieving sustainable development for all.

---

153 countries share transboundary rivers, lakes and aquifers.

Transboundary water cooperation can have a **positive effect on almost all 17 SDGs.**

---

[1] UN General Assembly Resolution 70/71, *Transforming our world: the 2030 Agenda for Sustainable Development*, 21 October 2015.

[2] Global Water Partnership Technical Advisory Committee. 2000. *Integrated Water Resources Management*, p. 22.

[3] See also SDG Indicator 6.5.1 Report.

[4] UN General Assembly Resolution 32/158, *United Nations Water Conference*, 19 December 1977; *Agenda 21: Programme of Action for Sustainable Development*, UN Doc. A/Conf.151/26 (1992); *Plan of Implementation of the World Summit on Sustainable Development*, UN Doc. A/Conf.199/L.7 (2002). Agenda 21, for instance, simply suggested that transboundary water cooperation "may be desirable in conformity with existing agreements and/or relevant arrangements, taking into account the interests of all riparian States concerned".

[5] See SDG Indicator 6.5.1 Report (n 3).

This firm commitment to implementing IWRM at all levels, including transboundary, spells out what is already implicit in the very notion of IWRM: namely the need for coordinated development and management. Such coordination must account for the indivisible characteristics of river, lake and aquifer systems, while at the same time overcoming the administrative and political boundaries that may not coincide with these natural systems. The importance of multi-level governance is therefore evident, as the appropriate law, policies and institutions must be in place at the national and subnational levels in order to implement cooperative arrangements effectively at the basin level.

1.2. Why is transboundary water cooperation important?

SDG target 6.5 is not alone in recognizing the critical contribution of transboundary water cooperation to achieving sustainable development for all. The growing momentum in support of transboundary water cooperation is evident in the entry into force of the Convention on the Law of the Non-navigational Uses of International Watercourses (Watercourses Convention) in 2014; the opening of the Convention on the Protection and Use of Transboundary Watercourses and International Lakes (Water Convention) to all United Nations Member States, which came into effect in 2016;[6] and the adoption of the International Law Commission's (ILC) Draft Articles on the Law of Transboundary Aquifers by the General Assembly in 2008.[7] The High-Level Panel on Water also recognized the importance of transboundary water cooperation as a "powerful tool for reaching the water-related SDG targets and the broader sustainable development goals"[8] and the Global High-Level Panel on Water and Peace stressed the need for countries to arrange transboundary water agreements, and called for widespread accession to both water conventions.[9]

The growing recognition of the importance of transboundary water cooperation in support of IWRM reflects two key realities: firstly, the extent to which countries rely upon transboundary waters to meet their domestic water needs, and secondly, the number of rivers, lakes and aquifers where arrangements for cooperation are still lacking.

Global water crises have repeatedly been recognized among the biggest threats facing the planet over the coming decades,[10] when demand for water is expected to increase by around 1 per cent per year due to pressures from population growth, economic development and changing consumption patterns.[11] Such pressures, together with impacts from climate change, will result in major challenges. It is estimated that two thirds of the population already live in areas that are potentially water-scarce for at least one month of the year.[12] Water pollution also constitutes a major threat to waters in Africa, Asia and Latin America, and further deterioration in water quality will negatively impact human health, the environment and sustainable development.[13] Any response to these challenges and threats must account for the fact that 153 countries share transboundary rivers, lakes and aquifers. The corresponding transboundary basins are home to over 2.8 billion people (42 per cent of the world's population), cover 62 million km^2 of the land on Earth (42 per cent), and account for 54 per cent of global river discharge.[14]

The lack of operational arrangements is a major barrier to addressing the world's water crises. While an estimated 450 transboundary water treaties have been adopted since 1820, many transboundary rivers, lakes and aquifers lack the necessary arrangements to support their sustainable development.[15]

---

[6] In 2018, Chad became the first country from outside the UNECE region to accede to the Convention.

[7] UN General Assembly Resolution 63/124, *The law of transboundary aquifers*, 11 December 2008.

[8] High Level Panel on Water, *Making Every Drop Count – An Agenda for Water Action*, https://sustainabledevelopment.un.org/content/documents/17825HLPW_Outcome.pdf (accessed 2 July 2018), p. 20.

[9] Global High-Level Panel on Water and Peace, *A Matter of Survival* (Geneva Water Hub 2017), p. 41.

[10] For example, the World Economic Forum's annual *Global Risks* report repeatedly highlights water among the top five global risks. See World Economic Forum, *The Global Risks Report 2018* (13th Edn, World Economic Forum 2018).

[11] Food and Agricultural Organization, AQUASTAT, http://fao.org/nr/water/aquastat/main/index.stm (accessed 2 July 2018).

[12] M. Mekonnen and A. Hoekstra. 2016. Four billion people facing severe water scarcity. *Science Advances*, Vol. 2, No. 2.

[13] *Id.*

[14] UNEP-DHI and UNEP. 2016. *Transboundary River Basins: Status and trends*, p. 2.

[15] See *infra* chapter three.

Figure 1: Transboundary river and lake basins, transboundary aquifers and international borders

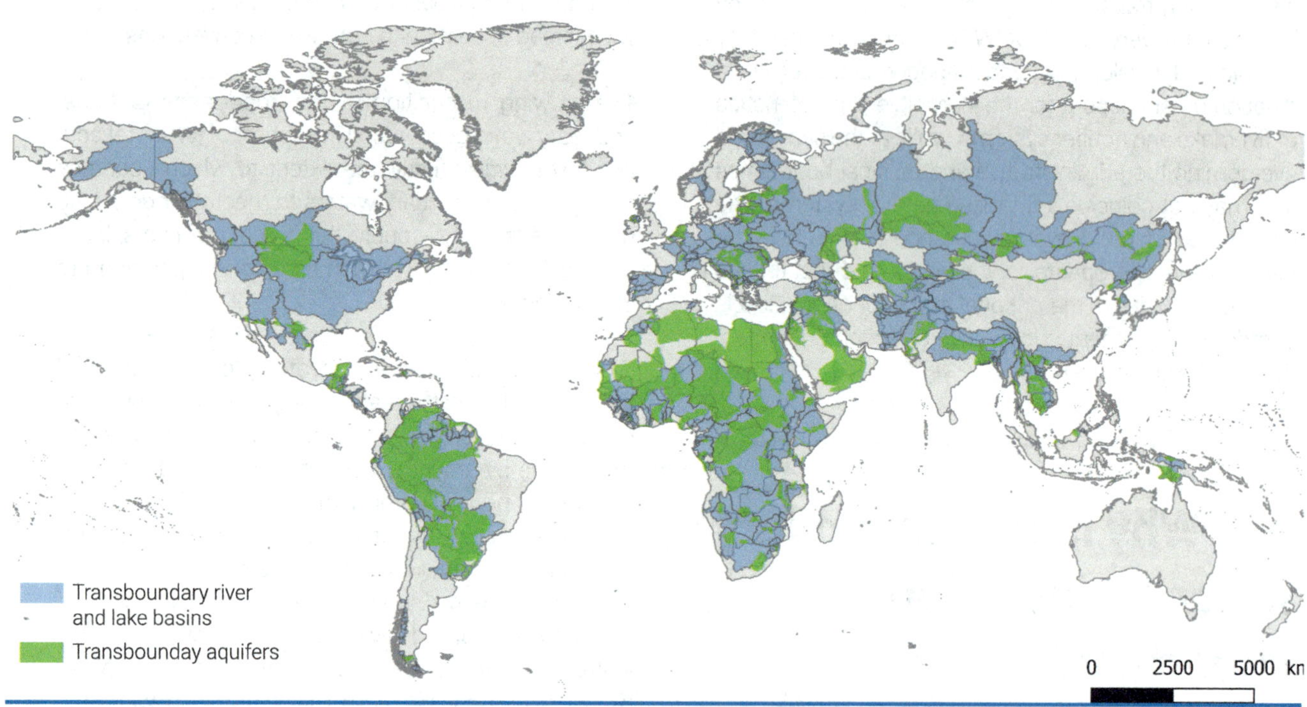

Source: UNESCO-IGRAC. 2015. Map of Transboundary Aquifers of the World. Scale 1:50 000 000. Paris, France (aquifers); UNEP and GEF, TWAP River Basins Data Portal: http://twap-rivers.org/indicators/ (accessed 2 July 2018) (river and lake basins)

1.3. Transboundary water cooperation and SDG linkages

A compelling argument in support of strengthening arrangements for transboundary water cooperation is their role in fostering multiple benefits beyond water. Transboundary water cooperation can, in fact, have a positive effect on almost all 17 SDGs. While international cooperation underpins many of the SDGs, target 6.5 is the only target that specifically references the need for transboundary cooperation, thereby offering an important means by which to further the "transboundary" elements that are fundamental to many SDGs including poverty (SDG 1), hunger (SDG 2), health and well-being (SDG 3), gender equality (SDG 5), water (SDG 6), energy (SDG 7), economic growth (SDG 8), infrastructure (SDG 9), reduced inequalities (SDG 10), climate action (SDG 13), and marine and ter-restrial ecosystems (SDG 14 and 15). Significant gains can therefore be made by coordinating SDG indicator 6.5.2 monitoring and analysis with the many associated indicators and targets, and exploring correlations between goals, target and indicators to capitalize on joint delivery.[16]

One example of these correlations is climate action (SDG 13) and transboundary water cooperation. Climate change will result in major impacts on water resources, including the increased frequency and intensity of floods and droughts, heightened water scarcity, intensified erosion and sedimentation, reduced glacier and snow cover, sea level rise, poorer water quality and degraded ecosystems.[17] Implementing IWRM at all appropriate levels is therefore critical to climate change adaptation. Cooperation over transboundary basins can help countries adapt to climate change by broadening knowledge and understanding of its likely impacts at the basin scale, enlarging the range of measures available for prevention, preparedness and recovery, and finding the most cost-effective solutions.[18]

---

[16] On linkages between SDG 6 and other SDGs, see UN-Water. 2016. *Water and Sanitation Interlinkages Across the 2030 Agenda for Sustainable Development*.

[17] Intergovernmental Panel on Climate Change. 2014. *Climate Change 2014: Synthesis Report*, p. 60.

[18] UNECE. 2009. *Guidance to Water and Adaptation to Climate Change*, p. 3.

[19] Lynette de Silva *et al.*, 'The Role of Women in Transboundary Water Dispute Resolution', in C. Fröhlich *et al.*, (eds), *Water Security Across the Gender Divide* (Springer 2018).

The implementation of SDG 5 (gender equality) also illustrates the links between transboundary water cooperation and other SDGs.[19] The extent to which gender objectives are currently developed and addressed at the transboundary (as well as national and subnational) level is considered to be relatively low.[20] Where appropriate, the membership, rules and procedures of joint bodies for transboundary water cooperation should be revised to promote gender equality and empower women in decision-making processes concerning transboundary water management. Similarly, any joint activity undertaken by countries related to transboundary cooperation provides an opportunity to mainstream gender aspects and apply gender assessments (see Box 1).

Joint bodies for transboundary water cooperation are an important means by which to advance several SDGs in a coordinated manner. For example, the Itaipu Binational Commission between Brazil and Paraguay, established in 1974 to develop and operate the Itaipu hydropower scheme, directly contributes to the provision of water (SDG 6) and energy (SDG 7) for all within the Paraná River Basin.[21] Additionally, through a wide range of sustainability projects, the Commission supports SDGs relating to low-income communities (SDG 1), sustainable agricultural production (SDG 2), traditional medicine (SDG 3), environmental education (SDG 4), participatory management (SDG 5 and 16), the creation of job opportunities (SDG 8), sustainable and resilient infrastructure (SDG 9), climate action (SDG 13), and conservation and biodiversity protection (SDG 15).

BOX 1

Gender-sensitive approaches to transboundary aquifers

The UNESCO-IHP Governance of Groundwater Resources in Transboundary Aquifers (GGRETA) project is applying a gender-sensitive assessment approach on three transboundary aquifers located in Central America, Southern Africa and Central Asia. The project has applied a pioneering methodological framework and key gender indicators developed by the UNESCO World Water Assessment Programme (WWAP). These have proved useful to understanding whether freshwater provision and allocation and ecosystems conservation are managed fairly and with a gender-equality focus.

In Southern Africa, the newly established joint mechanism for the governance of the Stampriet Transboundary Aquifer System (Botswana, Namibia and South Africa) has a gender working group that provides science-based gender data. These data are used to substantiate gender mainstreaming of national water policies and implement gender-transformative national and regional actions. In Central America, on-going activities such as tailored awareness-raising and training sessions are supporting the inclusion of gender issues in policies of local municipalities and entities sharing the Ocotepeque-Citala Transboundary Aquifer (El Salvador and Honduras). Discussions to establish a joint governance mechanism for the aquifer have made explicit reference to women's participation.

For further information on WWAP methodology, see http://unesco.org/new/en/natural-sciences/environment/water/wwap/water-and-gender/water-and-gender-toolkit/#c1430757, and for details on how it is applied in the GGRETA project, see http://unesdoc.unesco.org/images/0024/002452/245266e.pdf.

---

[20] SDG Indicator 6.5.1 (n 3), section 4.3
[21] See Itaipu Binacional, 'UNDESA and Itaipu Binacional launch the sustainable water and energy solutions partnership initiative', https://itaipu.gov.br/en/press-office/news/undesa-and-itaipu-binacional-launch-sustainable-water-and-energy-solutions-partner (accessed 2 July 2018).

1.4. Aims, objectives and outline

The purpose of this publication is to provide an overview of the results of the first monitoring exercise of SDG indicator 6.5.2. This overview is primarily based on an analysis of the data submitted by countries through their national reports. The publication highlights the current status and trends in transboundary water cooperation and considers whether the international community is on track to implement IWRM at all levels, especially transboundary, by 2030, as well as what support might be needed to meet this target by 2030. Given that this is the first time the SDG indicator 6.5.2 indicator methodology has been applied, the report also provides an opportunity to share experiences on its implementation, with a view to considering SDG indicator 6.5.2 monitoring going forward.

The report is structured around four chapters. Following this introduction, chapter two briefly outlines the SDG indicator 6.5.2 monitoring process, the role of the custodian agencies, and the strengths and limitations of this indicator. Chapter three presents the key findings from the first reporting cycle at the global and regional levels. In order to capture a broader range of transboundary cooperation, chapter three also explores the "operationality" criteria and considers the differing approaches that countries have taken. The final chapter analyses whether the international community is on track to achieving transboundary cooperation as called for by target 6.5, and what measures are needed to ensure that the target is met by 2030.

In presenting the status of transboundary water cooperation, it is envisaged that the report will be of value to a diverse readership. It should encourage shared learning and the exchange of experiences between Governments. Along similar lines, Governments, international organizations and others involved in transboundary water cooperative processes will be able to use the report to identify where their efforts would be best targeted. Governments that share transboundary basins, but that did not participate in the first reporting exercise, can discover how to engage in future reporting exercises. Similarly, in highlighting the lessons learned from the first reporting exercise, the report will be of value to experts and organizations that have an interest in supporting and analysing SDG monitoring and in fostering synergies across SDGs.

The reporting process and the role of custodian agencies

The Brahmaputra River originates on the Angsi Glacier in the Himalayas and flows into the Bay of Bengal. Photo: Jitendra Bajracharya/ Creative Commons

2.1. What is SDG indicator 6.5.2?

SDG indicator 6.5.2 measures the proportion of the transboundary basin area (river, lake or aquifer) within a country with an operational arrangement for water cooperation in place.[22] An "arrangement" might include a bilateral or multilateral treaty, convention, agreement or other formal arrangement among countries that provides a framework for cooperation on transboundary basins. The indicator is calculated based on:

- the total surface area of transboundary river or lake basins or aquifers within a country (in km^2)
- whether any transboundary river or lake basins or aquifers, or parts thereof, are covered by an arrangement for water cooperation and
- whether the arrangement(s) is "operational".

For an arrangement to be considered operational, all four of the following criteria must be met: i) there is a joint body or mechanism in place; ii) there are at least annual meetings between riparian countries; iii) a joint or coordinated water management plan has been established or joint objectives have been set; and iv) at least annual exchanges of data and information take place.[23]

Through these criteria, SDG indicator 6.5.2 measures more than the mere existence of an arrangement or joint body, instead considering the critical question of whether cooperation is operational. While formal structures offer an important stepping stone upon which to foster long-term cooperation, they may not always do so. For example, some arrangements are little more than "paper tigers", which may lack the necessary political support to guarantee their implementation.[24] Such arrangements may therefore lie dormant for many years.[25]

The establishment of joint bodies, regular meetings, data and information exchange, as well as the setting of joint plans and objectives, might be seen as fundamental, mutually reinforcing pre-requisites upon which more sophisticated cooperative activities in support of

KEY FACTS

SDG indicator 6.5.2 measures the **proportion of the transboundary basin area** (river, lake or aquifer) within a country with an **operational arrangement for water cooperation** in place.

The **107 responses** demonstrate a **strong commitment** to reporting data and information on the status of transboundary water cooperation.

---

[22] For further details, see Annex II.

[23] See *Step-by-step monitoring methodology for indicator 6.5.2*, http://unwater.org/app/uploads/2017/05/Step-by-step-methodology-6-5-2_Revision-2017-01-11_Final-1.pdf (accessed 2 July 2018).

[24] T. Bernauer. 2002. Explaining Success and Failure in International River Management. *Aquatic Sciences*, Vol. 64, No. 1, pp. 1-19.

[25] M. Zeitoun and J. Warner. 2006. Hydro-hegemony – a framework for analysis of trans-boundary water conflicts. *Water Policy*, Vol. 8, No. 5, pp. 435-460.

BOX 2

Calculation of the SDG indicator 6.5.2 value

$$\frac{A + C}{B + D} \times 100 = \underline{\quad}\%$$

[A] Total surface area of transboundary basins/sub-basins of rivers and lakes covered by operational arrangements within the territory of the country in km²
[B] Total surface area of transboundary basins of rivers and lakes within the territory of the country in km²
[C] Total surface area of transboundary aquifers covered by operational arrangements within the territory of a country in km²
[D] Total surface area of transboundary aquifers within the territory of a country in km²

IWRM can take place. For example, without a regular exchange of data and information, the effectiveness of any regular meetings would be seriously undermined, and any meaningful plans or objectives could not be set. This important relationship between the four criteria justifies the requirement that all four must be met.

The development of SDG indicator 6.5.2 builds upon, and can be compared to, other efforts to measure transboundary water cooperation.[26] Such efforts include initiatives to gather together legal instruments relating to transboundary basins;[27] to identify and delineate transboundary rivers, lakes and aquifers;[28] and more broadly to use different indicators – such as the existence of river basin organizations, certain legal principles, or conflict resolution mechanisms – as proxies to measure transboundary water cooperation.[29] Nevertheless, SDG indicator 6.5.2 represents the first time that countries themselves have reported on the operationality of their arrangements for cooperation within the wider SDG indicator framework. The results of the first SDG indicator 6.5.2 reporting exercise therefore provide a unique insight into the level of cooperation across the reporting countries, as well as an indication of the gaps that remain, both in terms of basins where arrangements are not operational or are lacking, and the countries for which reports are currently missing.

A group of children explore the frozen Syr Darya river (Baikonur). Photo: L Japrea/Creative Commons

[26] For a more detailed review of existing indicators, see M. McCracken. 2017. *Measuring transboundary cooperation: options for Sustainable Development Goal target 6.5.* GWP; and D Saruchera and Jonathan Lautze. 2015. *Measuring transboundary water cooperation: learning from the past to inform the sustainable development goals.* IWMI.
[27] See, for example, Oregon State University, International Freshwater Treaties Database, http://transboundarywaters.science.oregonstate.edu/content/international-freshwater-treaties-database (accessed 2 July 2018).
[28] IGRAC, Transboundary Aquifers of the World 2017, https://apps.geodan.nl/igrac/ggis-viewer/viewer/transboundary/public/default (accessed 2 July 2018).
[29] Lucia de Stefano *et al.* 2010. *Mapping the Resilience of International River Basins to Future Climate Change-induced Water Variability.* World Bank; UNEP-DHI and UNEP, n 14; Strategic Foresight Group. 2017. *Water Cooperation Quotient 2017;* Lucia de Stefano *et al.* 2017. Assessment of transboundary river basins for potential hydro-political tensions. *Global Environmental Change*, Vol. 45, pp. 35-46.

BOX 3

Limits of SDG indicator 6.5.2

SDG indicator 6.5.2 only measures the existence of operational arrangements, not their outcomes
The outcome of such cooperation, such as better water quality leading to improved human well-being, is beyond the scope of the indicator. However, SDG indicator 6.5.2 results can be analysed together with the results of other indicators, both within and outside the SDG framework, to ascertain correlations between operational arrangements and outcomes.

SDG indicator 6.5.2 does not measure cooperation in the absence of an operational arrangement.
While informal co-operative arrangements may be significant, operational arrangements offer a tangible indication of long-term commitment in support of IWRM implementation. At the same time, operational arrangements, while formal, may be both light in structure and flexible (see Chapter 3). Additionally, the four criteria used to determine whether an arrangement is operational, and the associated template for reporting on SDG indicator 6.5.2, can be analysed to ascertain evidence of cooperative activities falling short of being operational.

BOX 4

The origins of SDG indicator 6.5.2

On 6 March 2015, the United Nations Statistical Commission created an Inter-agency Expert Group on SDG Indicators (IAEG-SDGs) tasked with developing and implementing a global indicator framework for SDGs and their targets. In addition to the indicators themselves, the IAEG-SDGs also proposed custodian agencies for each indicator. These agencies are responsible for communicating with countries and coordinating country data; reviewing and validating data (where applicable); and disseminating the results of the data-gathering exercise to countries, international agencies and other stakeholders.

SDG indicator 6.5.2 on transboundary water cooperation was first introduced by UN-Water at the second IAEG-SDG meeting in Bangkok on 26–28 October 2015, on the basis that it "represents a significant increase in the aspiration regarding water management compared to previous international commitments". The indicator framework, including indicator 6.5.2, was agreed upon by the IAEG-SDGs at the forty-eighth session of the United Nations Statistical Commission in March 2017, and subsequently adopted by the United Nations General Assembly on 6 July 2017. UNECE and UNESCO were identified as co-custodian agencies for its implementation and development. The adoption of SDG indicator 6.5.2 by the United Nations General Assembly is the first time that a country-led instrument for measuring the status of transboundary water cooperation has been agreed upon at the global level.

The Danube, the world's most international river basin, with 19 countries sharing its basin. Photo: Andrew Moore/Creative Commons

2.2. The reporting template and the Water Convention

SDG indicator 6.5.2 provides countries with an opportunity to report on the status of transboundary cooperation from a national perspective. However, a single indicator can capture only certain aspects of a complex reality and cannot reflect the many activities related to transboundary water cooperation. The reporting template for SDG indicator 6.5.2 was therefore designed in a way that provided countries with the opportunity to both substantiate their calculation of the indicator and give additional information on complementary activities that they carry out in support of transboundary water cooperation. For specific basins and sub-basins, countries were invited to provide further information concerning their joint arrangements and bodies, and various activities in support of these governance structures, including the adoption of management plans and joint objectives, the exchange of data and information, joint monitoring, and the involvement of stakeholders in transboundary water management. More generally, countries were invited to comment on the laws and policies that they have in place at the national level to support transboundary water cooperation and to consider the main challenges and achievements facing the country in cooperating on transboundary waters.[30] As reflected in chapter three of this report, this supplementary information offers more context, explanation and justification for the SDG indicator 6.5.2 calculations that countries provided.

When designing the template for reporting under SDG indicator 6.5.2, the custodian agencies referred to the template developed for reporting under the Water Convention.[31] The latter had been developed in 2014-2015 through an intergovernmental process reflecting the needs and expectations of countries, both Parties and non-Parties to the Water Convention, and was subsequently revised in October 2016 to incorporate information related to SDG indicator 6.5.2. The Parties to the Water Convention therefore aligned both exercises by essentially developing a common template to enable the 41 State Parties to report under the Water Convention and SDG indicator 6.5.2 at the same time, and in a way that avoids duplication, i.e. only one template is completed and submitted for both exercises.

---

[30] The template is included in Annex II.
[31] In November 2015, at the seventh session of the Meeting of the Parties to the Water Convention, a decision was made to introduce regular reporting under the Convention (Decision VII/2, in UNECE, *Report of the Meeting of the Parties on its seventh session*, UN Doc. ECE/MP.WAT/49).

BOX 5

The Convention on the Protection and Use of Transboundary Watercourses and International Lakes

The Convention on the Protection and Use of Transboundary Watercourses and International Lakes, also known as the Water Convention or Helsinki Convention, is a key United Nations legal and intergovernmental institutional framework promoting the quantity, quality and sustainable use of transboundary surface-water and groundwater resources by facilitating and strengthening cooperation.

The Convention, which is serviced by the United Nations Economic Commission for Europe, was originally negotiated in 1992 as a pan-European regional framework. It was subsequently amended to become global in its reach. As of 2016, all United Nations Member States can accede to it. In July 2018, the Convention counts 42 Parties, including almost all countries in the pan-European region sharing transboundary waters, and Chad, which is the first Party from Africa.

The Convention, which embodies and builds upon the main principles of international water law, requires its Parties to enter into specific agreements or arrangements on their transboundary waters and establish joint bodies (such as river basin organizations) for their management (article 9). The Convention also requires riparian countries to exchange data and information (articles 6 and 13) and elaborate plans, programmes and objectives (articles 9, 11, 12 and 14).

BOX 6

The benefits of the reporting process from a country perspective

In July and October 2017, UNECE and UNESCO invited all countries sharing transboundary basins to reflect on the reporting process. In addition, a technical meeting, which brought together over 50 country representatives to review the reporting process, was held in Budapest in January 2018. Countries identified several benefits from the reporting process, including:

— The reporting process offered an opportunity to focus political attention on the importance of transboundary water cooperation;
— Reporting allowed countries to gather information that was scattered between different authorities and thereby to gain a shared vision and understanding of the issue at the national level;
— Reporting allowed countries to take stock of progress and identify basins where cooperative arrangements might need to be negotiated or where existing arrangements might need to be strengthened;
— Reporting offered the opportunity to initiate an inter-sectoral dialogue on transboundary water cooperation across governmental sectors, and in some instances beyond government;
— Reporting proved to be a useful means by which to reflect on the status of transboundary water cooperation between riparian countries and at the basin level. In this regard, some countries found it valuable to exchange reports or parts thereof with countries sharing one or several basins. In some instances, joint bodies proved a useful channel for exchanging draft reports.

Further information on the Budapest technical meeting to review reporting is available at: https://unece.org/index.php?id=47476.

2.3. SDG indicator 6.5.2 responses and the review process

Early in 2017, all 153 countries sharing transboundary waters were invited by the custodian agencies to report under SDG indicator 6.5.2. This invitation resulted in 107 responses (i.e. a 70 per cent response rate). This is outstanding for a newly introduced SDG indicator and demonstrates a strong commitment from countries to reporting data and information on the status of transboundary water cooperation.

When national SDG indicator 6.5.2 reports were submitted to the custodian agencies, several checks were made. Firstly, based on the data provided by the countries, the custodian agencies verified whether there were any mistakes in the calculation of the indicator. Secondly, the custodian agencies checked for consistency between the different sections of the reporting template and the basins reported in the SDG indicator calculation. For example, the custodian agencies checked for consistency between the basins that a country classified as operational, and the country's responses to questions in the template related to the operationality criteria. Thirdly, where a country identified an aquifer as falling within the scope of a transboundary river or lake basin arrangement, the custodian agencies checked, where possible, if the border of the transboundary aquifer was encompassed within the river or lake basin.[32] Fourthly, to be sure of the official nature of the information, the custodian agencies checked whether national reports had been signed by a country representative. Where necessary, the custodian agencies sought clarification from countries.

The indicator calculation includes a component relating to river and lake basins, and a component linked to aquifers. An overall indicator value for SDG indicator 6.5.2 could only be considered if both components were reported and the aforementioned checks were satisfied. Therefore, while 107 responses were received from countries, not all reports could be included in the initial analysis because requests for clarification from several countries are still pending.

Given that the indicator calculation includes a river and lake basin component, and an aquifer component, it has sometimes been possible to present one of the components even where it is not possible to present the overall SDG indicator 6.5.2 value.[33]

Where data were provided by countries, the United Nations Economic Commission for Europe (UNECE) and the United Nations Educational, Scientific and Cultural Organization (UNESCO) relied upon those data in relation to both the rivers, lakes and aquifers listed, and their estimated surface area. Where national data sources proved difficult to find, the two custodians encouraged countries to consult global sources, such as the Transboundary Waters Assessment Programme's (TWAP) data portal and UNESCO–International Hydrological Programme's (IHP) International Shared Aquifer Resources Management initiative (ISARM).[34] The initial reporting exercise demonstrated that there were often discrepancies between these global data sources and the data provided by countries, especially in relation to transboundary aquifers. In cooperation with countries, the custodian agencies tried to resolve any discrepancies between international and national data sources, although ultimately, the reporting was country driven and only the data provided by countries were used to calculate SDG indicator 6.5.2.

Discrepancies also arose where the countries sharing the same basin had different interpretations or conflicting data on the transboundary nature of a basin, its surface area, the relationship between surface water and groundwater, and whether they considered a basin to be operational. Attempts were made to reconcile differing interpretations between States but, as noted above, ultimately the reporting was conducted at the national level, and only data provided by each country were used to calculate the SDG indicator 6.5.2 value for that country. Any discrepancies offer important insights into country perspectives.

A further challenge was that data on transboundary aquifers, such as a detailed delineation, often appeared to be lacking at the national level. As countries might only have partial information for the aquifer, e.g. on the part within their country, some countries have only included some of their transboundary aquifers in the assessment. Moreover, not having full coverage of transboundary aquifers may have resulted in some countries deciding not to report. The

---

[32] Such a check was only possible in cases where the reported aquifers were consistent with the ISARM database (n 28), which serves as a basis for localizing the aquifers.
[33] In some cases, the basic information to calculate an indicator value for aquifers was not presented in the national report (e.g. no list of all transboundary aquifers with related surface area), but the full indicator value could still be determined based on the information contained in the reports and the fact that the national value was 100 per cent full cooperation or 0 per cent no cooperation.
[34] See UNEP-DHI and UNEP (n 14) and IGRAC (n 28).

BOX 7

The challenge of defining aquifer boundaries (TWAP Groundwater Final Report)

Worldwide studies of transboundary aquifers (TBAs) started in around 2000, with UNESCO-IHP's launch of ISARM. The first map providing a global overview of TBAs (Groundwater Resources of the World: Transboundary Aquifer Systems) was produced under the framework of the UNESCO WHYMAP programme (Struckmeier *et al.*, 2006) and showed the approximate location of about 100 TBAs. Since then, UNESCO has gradually developed knowledge of the world's TBAs and disseminates scientific knowledge. TBAs have gradually been better defined and information has been shared with Member States and the international community through regular map updates. In 2015, a more detailed map identifying 592 TBAs was produced.

Mapping TBAs (or aquifers in general) is not straightforward. Accurate mapping requires costly and in-depth studies into the three-dimensional geological deposits and structures to define the hydrogeological units within these structures/deposits. This requires geological mapping, borehole information on geology, borehole yield and water quality, pumping tests to establish aquifer characteristics, geophysical studies, etc. Even when all these data are available, defining the three-dimensional boundaries of a TBA or aquifer system is still not straightforward. Different countries might use different criteria to define hydrogeological units, or their base maps might not have been harmonized. In many cases, the delineation is based on the mapping of the outcrop of the aquifer. For regions where data on hydrogeology are not available, the boundaries of aquifers may even have to be inferred from topographical features such as surface water divides. Boundaries might also change over time as more detailed knowledge becomes available. For example, an aquifer originally reported as a single-layer transboundary aquifer might later be defined as a transboundary aquifer system when individual aquifers/ aquifer layers have been mapped. (UNESCO-IHP and UNEP, 2016)

Struckmeier, W. F. *et al.* 2006. WHYMAP and the World Map of Transboundary Aquifer Systems at the scale of 1: 50 000 000 (Special Edition for the 4th World Water Forum, Mexico City, March 2006). BGR Hannover, Hannover, Germany and UNESCO, Paris, France.

UNESCO-IHP and UNEP. 2016. Transboundary Aquifers and Groundwater Systems of Small Island Developing States: Status and Trends. United Nations Environment Programme (UNEP), Nairobi.

challenges faced in reporting on transboundary aquifers can explain why some well-documented cases of transboundary aquifer cooperation in the scientific literature are not reflected in the national reports. Therefore, it is envisaged that in the framework of future reporting on SDG indicator 6.5.2, data on aquifers will gradually improve.

Figure 2 provides an overview of the number of responses received, the number of reports where, in accordance with the process described above, further clarification is still needed, and the number of countries sharing transboundary basins that did not submit a report. The following chapter explores the results in greater detail.

Figure 2: Overview of the number of responses received, the number of reports where further clarification is still needed, and the number of countries sharing transboundary basins that did not submit a report

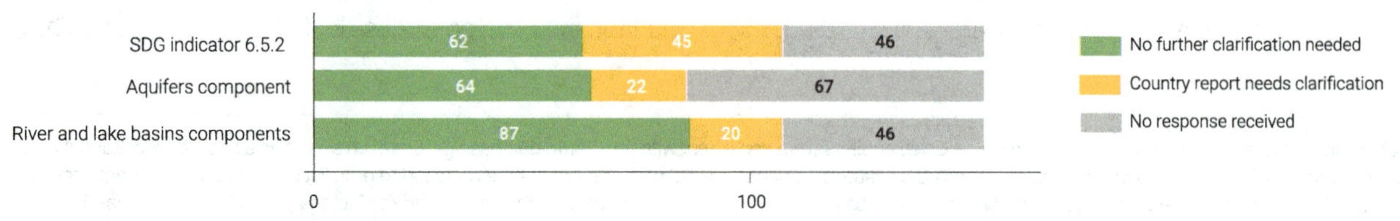

3

Assessing progress in transboundary water cooperation at the global and regional levels

The Niagara river forms part of the border between Canada and the United States. Photo: Shutter Photo/Creative Commons

This chapter explores the results of the first SDG indicator 6.5.2 monitoring exercise by first looking at the global level and then at each SDG regional grouping ("SDG regions"), namely Central and Southern Asia, Eastern and South-Eastern Asia, Europe and Northern America, Latin America and the Caribbean, Northern Africa and Western Asia, and sub-Saharan Africa.[35] In addition to presenting data on SDG indicator 6.5.2, where appropriate, additional data sources are used to supplement the data available for the overall indicator value. Finally, and based on the responses in the reporting template, the chapter provides a thematic analysis of each of the criteria for operationality in order to capture the diversity of operational arrangements, and to consider arrangements that fall short of the operationality criteria.

KEY FACTS

More effort is needed to **encourage countries to report on SDG indicator 6.5.2**, especially across the Asian region.

Only **17 countries** have all their transboundary basins covered by operational arrangements, and **12 of the countries** that reported have no operational arrangements in place.

Cooperation over **transboundary river and lake basins** is more widespread than cooperation over **aquifers**.

3.1. Global progress in transboundary water cooperation

3.1.1. Overview of SDG indicator 6.5.2 value

The "overall indicator value" (SDG indicator 6.5.2 for both river and lake basins, and aquifers) is available for 62 countries, which corresponds to 41 per cent of the 153 countries that share transboundary basins. Figure 3 shows that these 62 countries are spread over several regions, although some regions are better represented than others: 56 per cent of countries sharing transboundary basins in Northern America and Europe; 50 per cent for Latin America and the Caribbean; 47 per cent for sub-Saharan Africa; 33 per cent for Northern Africa and Western Asia; 28 per cent for Central and Southern Asia; and 8 per cent for Eastern and South-Eastern Asia. These percentages show that more effort is needed to encourage countries to report on SDG indicator 6.5.2, especially across the Asian region.

While it has therefore not been possible during the first reporting exercise to provide an overall indicator value for many countries that share transboundary basins,

---

[35] Two SDG regions have been excluded from the analysis because they either do not have any transboundary basins (Australia and New Zealand), or only a few transboundary basins exist, such as in the case of Oceania, where Papua New Guinea, which did not submit a national SDG 6.5.2 indicator report, is the only country sharing transboundary basins. The SDG regions of Central and Southern Asia, and Eastern and South-Eastern Asia, have been combined due to the limited number of countries that reported across both regions. For a list of countries per SDG region, see https://unstats.un.org/sdgs/indicators/regional-groups/ (accessed 2 July 2018).

Figure 3: National level of cooperation on transboundary water, and countries where further clarification is still needed

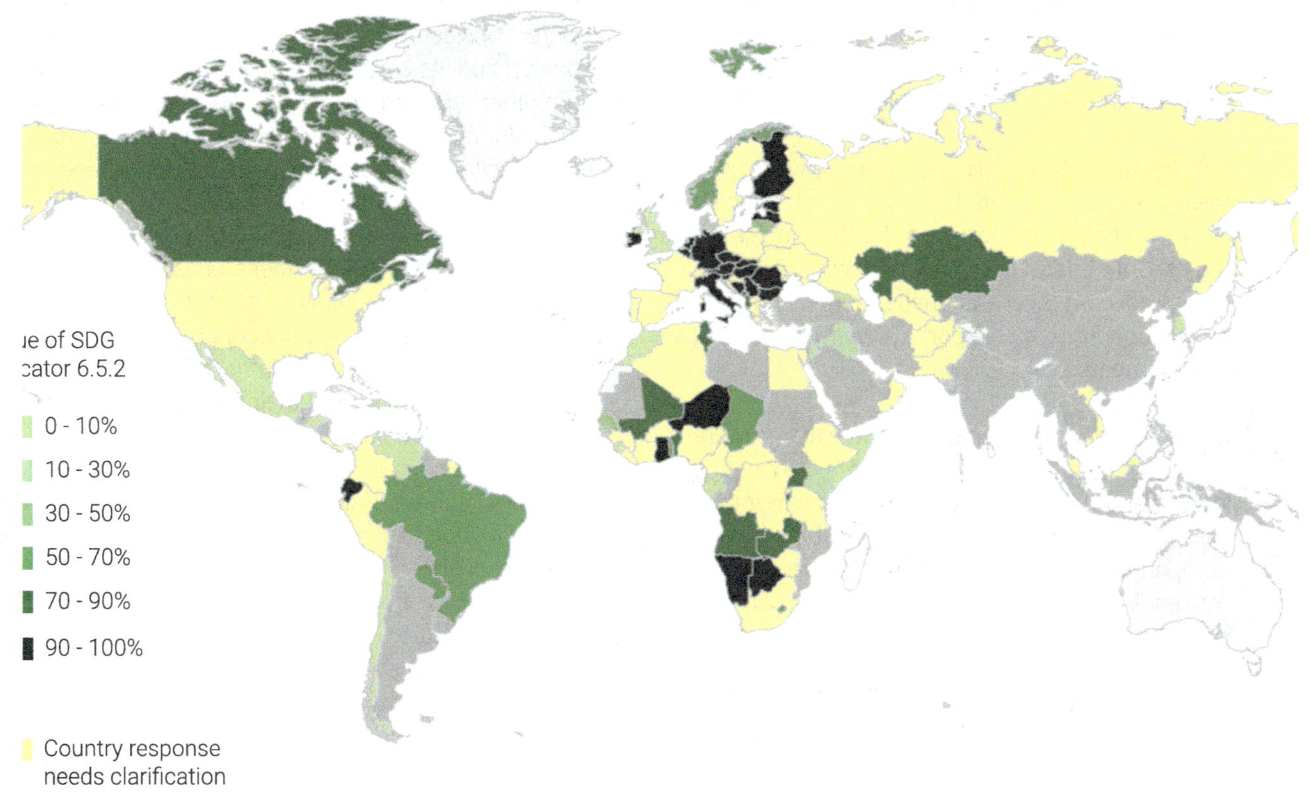

the 62 countries included offer a valuable insight into the status of transboundary water cooperation.[36] Moreover, while reporting occurs at the national level, the transboundary basins referred to by the 62 countries stretch across the territories of countries that are not included. This means, for example, that out of the 286 transboundary river basins listed in the TWAP database, only 101 river basins (or 35 per cent of the world's transboundary river basins) are shared exclusively by the 91 countries where the SDG indicator 6.5.2 value is not available. This would suggest that SDG indicator 6.5.2 reporting provides partial data on roughly two thirds of the world's transboundary river basins.

Figure 4: National level of cooperation on transboundary water, and countries where further clarification is still needed

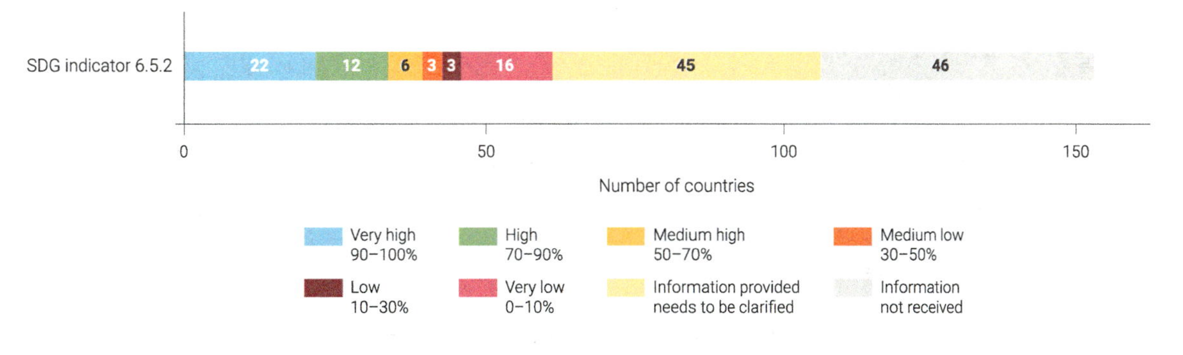

<hr>

[36] See UNEP-DHI and UNEP (n 14).

The overall indicator value of 59 per cent, based on data from the aforementioned 62 countries (see Figure 5), masks significant variation across these 62 countries. Figure 4 provides a breakdown of the overall indicator value across several percentage thresholds.

This finding of 59 per cent coverage across the countries that have reported suggests that significant effort is still needed to reach the SDG indicator 6.5 target. Only 17 countries have all their transboundary basins covered by operational arrangements, and 12 of the countries that reported have no operational arrangements in place.

An additional cause for concern is the status of transboundary water cooperation within the 91 countries where an SDG 6.5.2 indicator value is currently unavailable. In this respect, insights can be provided by comparing the results of SDG 6.5.2 indicator reporting with earlier assessments – although none of the previous assessments have measured the operationality of arrangements. One of the closest assessments is the analysis of legal frameworks conducted by TWAP.[37] The TWAP analysis indicated that, of the 91 countries not represented in the SDG 6.5.2 indicator calculation, 50 have no specific legal framework in place for the 148 transboundary river basins that they share.

It is also possible to compare the results of SDG indicator 6.5.2 with the transboundary questions that were considered in SDG indicator 6.5.1.[38] Such an analysis paints a similar picture. Out of the 128 countries that reported on transboundary waters for SDG indicator 6.5.1, only 32 per cent claim to have arrangements either fully or mostly implemented, and only 37 per cent claim that the mandate of any organizational framework is either fully fulfilled or mostly fulfilled. In responding to these questions, countries were asked to assess only their most important transboundary basins in terms of economic, social or environmental value to the country. If States had been asked to comment on all their transboundary basins, the results would have been lower.

The results of 6.5.1 and 6.5.2 indicators reporting, as well as related assessments, such as TWAP, therefore paint a consistent message that efforts are needed in approximately two thirds of the world's transboundary basins to ensure that, where appropriate, operational arrangements are in place.

Figure 5: Average national proportion of transboundary basin area covered by an operational arrangement and national data point for each country, where SDG 6.5.2 is available

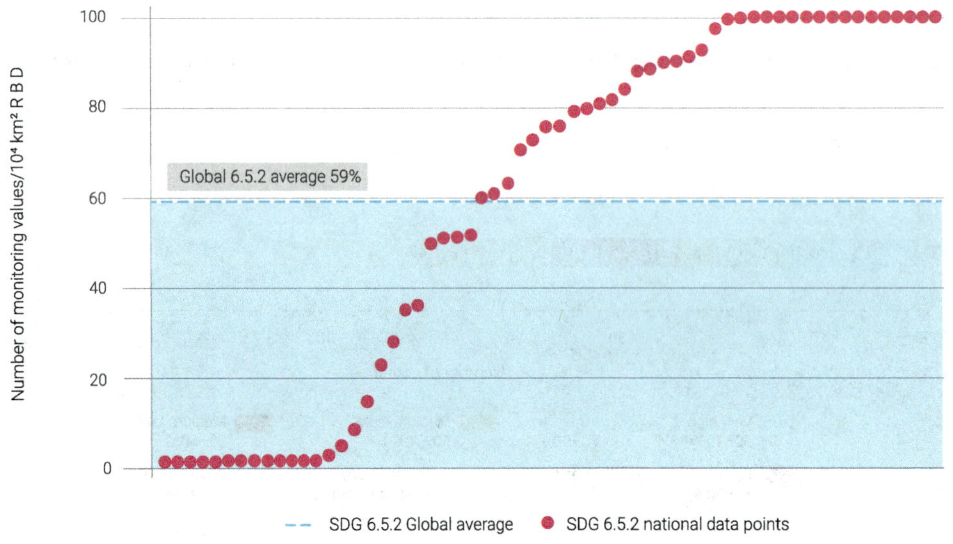

---

[37] See UNEP-DHI and UNEP (n 14).
[38] SDG indicator 6.5.1 Report (n 3).

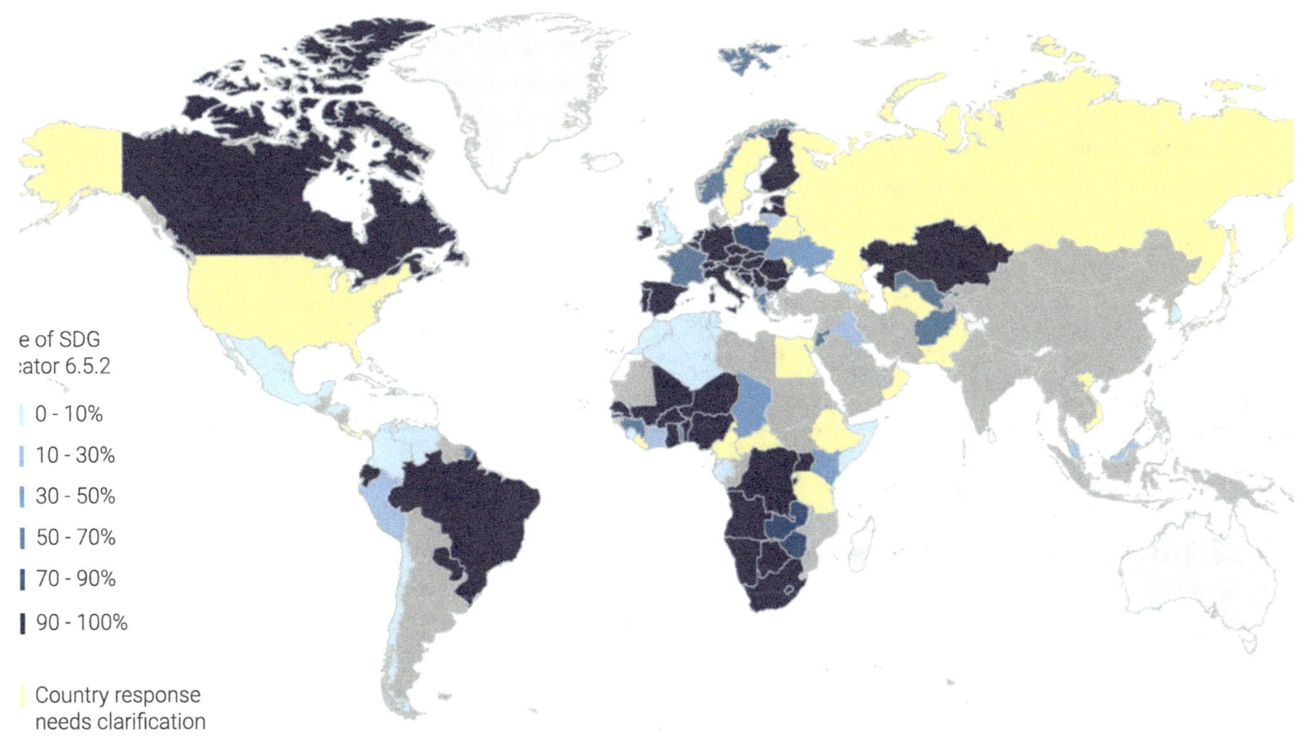

3.1.2. SDG indicator 6.5.2 for river and lake basins

In terms of transboundary river and lake basins, it is possible to provide an indicator value for 84 countries, which represents 55 per cent of all countries sharing transboundary waters. As Figure 6 shows, the value for river and lake basins is calculated for countries from across most SDG regions – although some regions are more strongly represented than others: the value is available for 79 per cent of countries sharing transboundary river and lake basins in Northern America and Europe; 64 per cent for sub-Saharan Africa; 50 per cent for Latin America and the Caribbean; 33 per cent for Northern African and Western Asia; 25 per cent for Central and Southern Asia; and 17 per cent for Eastern and South-Eastern Asia.

For the 84 countries represented, the value for transboundary river and lake basins is 64 per cent, which is higher than the overall indicator value (59 per cent). This shows that cooperation over transboundary river and lake basins is more widespread than cooperation over aquifers.

As with the overall indicator value, this average masks significant variation across the 84 countries represented (see Figure 7). For instance, 42 countries report having very high levels of operational arrangements in place, while 19 countries report very low levels of operational arrangements.

The results also show that across regions, there are many examples of operational arrangements between countries sharing transboundary river and lake basins. High levels of cooperation are particularly evident in Europe and Northern America, and sub-Saharan Africa. Out of 47 countries that reported having at least 70 per cent of their transboundary river and lake basin area covered by operational arrangements, 53 per cent can be found in Europe and 38 per cent in sub-Saharan Africa. The remaining four countries come from Latin America (Brazil, Ecuador and Paraguay), and Central Asia (Kazakhstan). Out of the 23 countries that report having less than 30 per cent of their transboundary river and lake basin area covered by operational arrangements, eight countries can be found in Latin America, six countries in Northern Africa and Western Asia, five countries in sub-Saharan Africa and four countries in Europe.

Figure 7: Global breakdown of the number of countries sharing river and lake basins and level of transboundary water cooperation

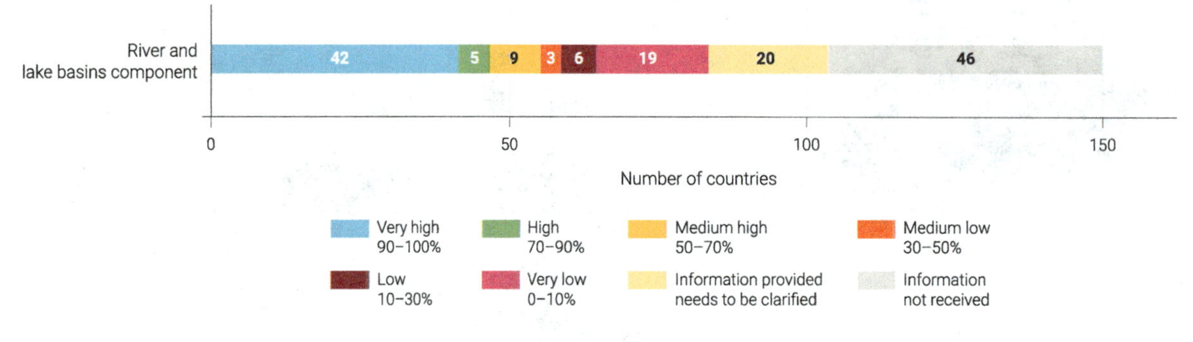

3.1.3. SDG 6.5.2 for transboundary aquifers

For the transboundary aquifer component of SDG indicator 6.5.2, data are available for 61 countries. As noted previously, the relatively low number of countries where aquifer-specific data are available reflects two key factors: namely the lack of knowledge and understanding of the physical characteristics of transboundary aquifers among riparian countries, and the limited number of arrangements for cooperation that have been developed for aquifers. As Figure 8 shows, the SDG 6.5.2 indicator calculation for transboundary aquifers covers countries from across several regions. The calculation is available for 58 per cent of countries that share transboundary aquifers in Europe and Northern America; 43 per cent for sub-Saharan Africa; 41 per cent for Latin American and the Caribbean; 33 per cent for Western Asia and Northern Africa; and 8 per cent for both Central and Southern Asia, and Eastern and South-Eastern Asia, combined.

Figure 8: National level of cooperation on transboundary aquifers, and countries where further clarification is still needed

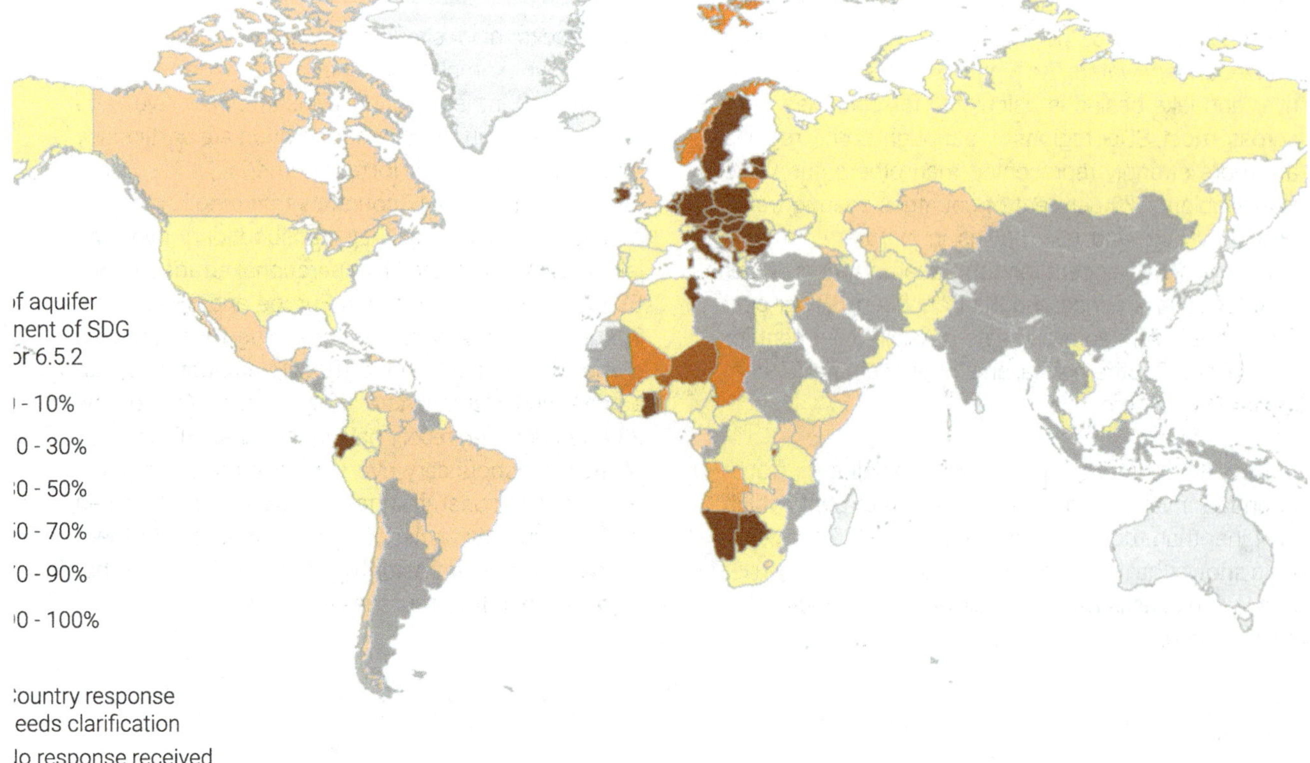

Figure 9: Global breakdown of the number of countries sharing aquifers and level of transboundary water cooperation

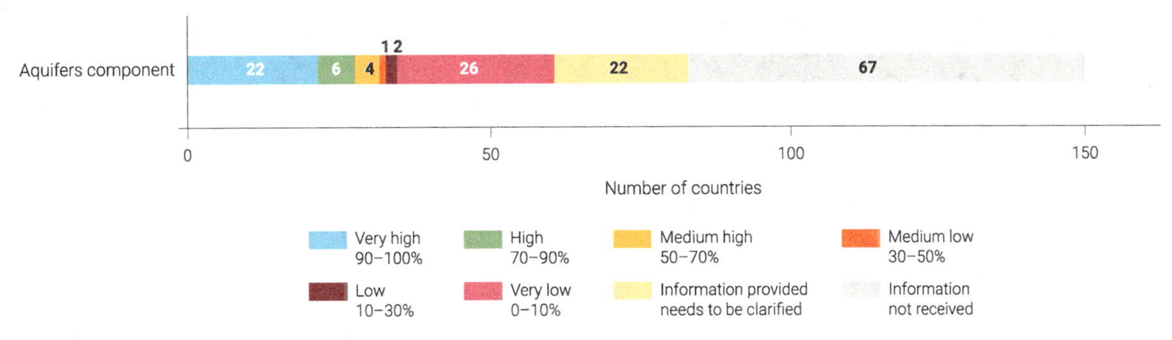

Based on these 61 countries, the indicator value for transboundary aquifers is 48 per cent, which is lower than the full value for the overall indicator (59 per cent). As with the overall indicator value, this average masks significant variation across the 61 countries represented (see Figure 9). Only 18 of the countries that were considered report that all their transboundary aquifer area is covered by operational arrangements. Most of these countries are in Europe; the remainder come from sub-Saharan Africa (Botswana and Namibia), Northern Africa (Tunisia), and Latin America (Ecuador). Countries recording low levels of operational arrangements for transboundary aquifers are spread across regions, with nine situated in sub-Saharan Africa (Angola, Gabon, Gambia, Kenya, Lesotho, Senegal, Somalia, Uganda and Zambia); eight situated in Latin America (Brazil, Chile, Dominican Republic, El Salvador, Honduras, Mexico, Paraguay and Venezuela); six situated in Northern Africa and Western Asia (Armenia, Georgia, Iraq, Jordan, Morocco and Qatar); three situated in Northern America and Europe (Canada, Montenegro and the United Kingdom); and one situated in Eastern Asia (Republic of Korea).

Most operational arrangements related to transboundary aquifers are combined agreements that cover both river or lake basins, and aquifers. As a direct consequence, countries with a high indicator value for river and lake basins tend to also score highly for the indicator value related to aquifers. For instance, the 2002 Scheldt Agreement between Belgium, France and the Netherlands concerns the protection and use of the waters in the International Scheldt River Basin District.[39] In adopting the term "International River Basin District", the 2002 Scheldt Agreement follows the practice of many agreements in Europe that were adopted following the entry into force of the 2000 EU Water Framework Directive.[40] The Scheldt River Basin District is accordingly defined as "the Scheldt river basin and the associated groundwaters and coastal waters".[41] In cases where groundwater is included in transboundary river basin arrangements or "combined" agreements, it is often difficult to assess the extent to which the provisions for cooperation effectively focus on aquifers and groundwater.

The countries of the Orange-Senqu River Basin (Botswana, Lesotho, Namibia and South Africa) have developed a novel approach to groundwater management. Despite the 2000 Orange-Senqu Agreement not explicitly referring to groundwater, the Parties have established a multi-country cooperation mechanism to manage the Stampriet aquifer, under the auspices of the Orange-Senqu River Basin Commission.[42]

[39] See River Scheldt Agreement, 3 October 2002, http://isc-cie.org/images/Documents/ACC_GENT_Scheldeverdrag.pdf, preamble (accessed 2 July 2018). Unofficial translation available at http://isc-cie.org/images/Documents/ACC_GENT_SCHELDT_AGREEMENT.pdf

[40] Directive 2000/60/EC of 23 October 2000 establishing a framework for community action in the field of water policy (EU Water Framework Directive), http://eur-lex.europa.eu/legal-content/EN/TXT/HTML/?uri=CELEX:32000L0060&from=EN (accessed 2 July 2018). Article 3(1) of the EU Water Framework Directive provides that "Member States shall identify the individual river basins lying within their national territory and, for the purposes of this Directive, shall assign them to individual river basin districts. Small river basins may be combined with larger river basins or joined with neighboring small basins to form individual river basin districts where appropriate. Where groundwaters do not fully follow a particular river basin, they shall be identified and assigned to the nearest or most appropriate river basin district. Coastal waters shall be identified and assigned to the nearest or most appropriate river basin district or districts."

[41] Scheldt Agreement (n 39), Art. 1(d).

[42] Agreement on the Establishment of the Orange-Senqu River Commission, 3 November 2000, https://iea.uoregon.edu/treaty-text/2000-orangesenqucommissionentxt (accessed 2 July 2018).

3.2. Regional progress in transboundary water cooperation

3.2.1. Central, Eastern, Southern and South-Eastern Asia

Of the 30 countries in Central, Eastern, Southern and South-Eastern Asia, 24 share transboundary river basins.[43] Reports were received from nine of these 24 countries. Due to the need for further clarification, mainly related to a lack of data on transboundary aquifers, the overall indicator value can only be calculated for two of the nine countries: Kazakhstan (72 per cent) and the Republic of Korea (0 per cent). For the calculation of river and lake basins, data are available for three further countries – Afghanistan, Malaysia and Uzbekistan.

Kazakhstan and the Republic of Korea have very different hydro-geological characteristics and the cooperation that they have developed with their neighbours is closely linked to their overall political relationships. For example, the only transboundary basins that the Republic of Korea shares are with the Democratic People's Republic of Korea, namely the Han River Basin, which has an area of 33,000 km² and is home to a population of 17,758,000;[44] and the Middle of Korea Peninsula Aquifer, which has an area of 17,000 km².[45] No operational arrangements are currently in place between the two countries.[46]

In contrast, Kazakhstan reports seven transboundary river and lake basins, and 15 transboundary aquifers. These basins are shared with several countries: China, Kyrgyzstan, Russian Federation, Tajikistan and Uzbekistan. Kazakhstan considers that operational arrangements are in place for all its transboundary river and lake basins. Specific arrangements exist for the Chu and Talas River Basins, and for the Amu Darya and Syr Darya River Basins;[47] and bilateral agreements on the other basins have been entered into with China and Russia.[48] Kazakhstan reports that none of its 15 transboundary aquifers are covered by an operational arrangement.

Of the three other countries where data are available for transboundary river and lake basins, Afghanistan reports that 52 per cent of its basin area is covered by operational arrangements, compared to 13 per cent in Malaysia and 59 per cent in Uzbekistan. Transboundary water cooperation in Afghanistan centres on the 1973 Helmand River Water Treaty with Iran, which has had a chequered history of implementation. In the case of Malaysia, a joint committee for the Golok River has been fostering cooperation since 1979, and is considered operational.[49] Meanwhile, Uzbekistan considers that operational arrangements are in place for the Amu Darya and Syr Darya Rivers. Afghanistan, Malaysia and Uzbekistan highlight that since data related to their transboundary aquifers are lacking, no overall value for SDG indicator 6.5.2 can be provided for the countries.

Beyond the cases reported in the national reports, there are notable examples of transboundary water cooperation across these two SDG regions. However, of the agreements that are in place, few adopt a basin-wide approach, or not all basin States are party to them.[50] For instance, the upstream States of the Mekong River Basin (China and Myanmar) are not party to the 1995 Mekong Agreement – although despite not being members, both countries cooperate with the lower Mekong States through the Mekong River Commission. Another example is the Ganges-Meghna-Brahmaputra River Basin, where several bilateral arrangements have been entered into, but basin-wide arrangements are currently lacking. Additionally, several major transboundary basins in Asia are lacking any arrangements for cooperation, such as the Salween River Basin between China, Myanmar and Thailand; the Irrawaddy River Basin between China, India and Myanmar; and the Red River Basin between China and Vietnam. Collectively, these three basins are home to an estimated population of over 54 million.[51]

---

[43] UNEP-DHI and UNEP (n 29).

[44] UNEP-DHI and UNEP (n 29).

[45] IGRAC (n 28).

[46] Laure-Elise Maynard, 'Fostering cooperation over the Han river between North and South Korea – Is the UN Watercourses Convention the appropriate instrument?'. Journal of Water Law (forthcoming).

[47] Agreement between the Government of the Kazakh Republic and the Government of the Kyrgyz Republic on the Use of Water Management Facilities of Intergovernmental Status on the Rivers Chu and Talas, 21 January 2000, http://unece.org/fileadmin/DAM/env/water/Chu-Talas/ChuTalas_Agreement_ENG.pdf (accessed 2 July 2018); and Agreement between the Republic of Kazakhstan, the Kyrgyz Republic, the Republic of Tajikistan, Turkmenistan and the Republic of Uzbekistan on Cooperation in the Field of Joint Management on Utilization and Protection of Water Resources from Interstate Sources, 18 February 1992, http://icwc-aral.uz/statute1.htm (accessed 2 July 2018).

[48] Agreement between the Government of the Republic of Kazakhstan and the Government of the People's Republic of China on Cooperation in the Use and Protection of Transboundary Rivers, 12 September 2001, http://cawater-info.net/library/eng/l/kazakhstan_china.pdf (accessed 2 July 2018); Agreement between Russia and Kazakhstan on Joint Use and Protection of Transboundary Waters, 7 September 2010.

[49] See Malaysia-Thailand Joint Committee for the Golok River Basin, http://h2o.water.gov.my/golok/main.html (accessed 2 July 2018).

[50] UNEP et al. 2009. *Hydropolitical Vulnerability and Resilience along International Waters.*

[51] UNEP-DHI and UNEP (n 14).

Figure 10: Central, Eastern, Southern & South-Eastern Asia: national level of cooperation on transboundary water, river and lake basins, and aquifers, and countries where further clarification is still needed

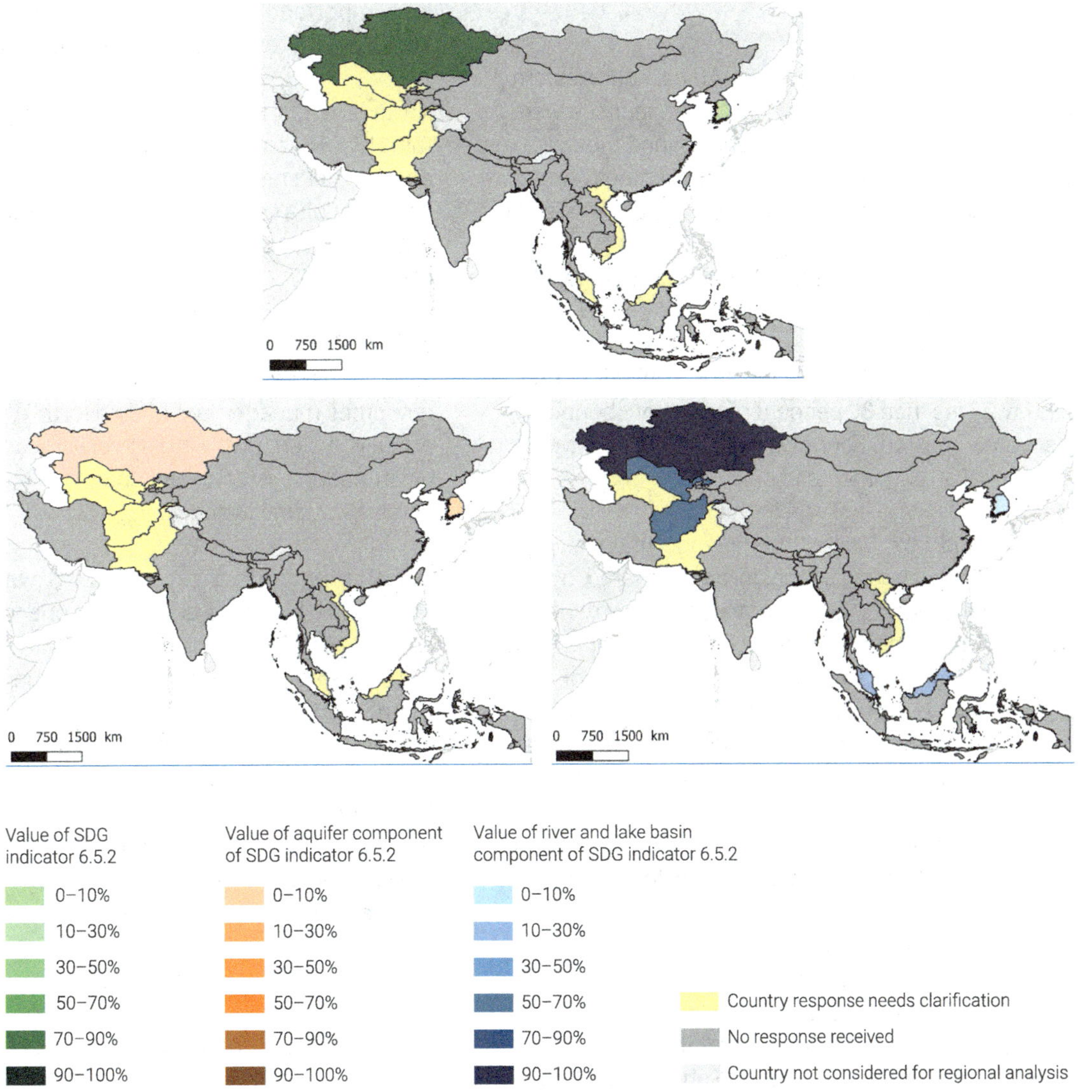

Figure 11: Central, Eastern, Southern & South-Eastern Asia: breakdown of the number of countries sharing waters and level of cooperation on transboundary water for SDG indicator 6.5.2, aquifers, and river and lake basins

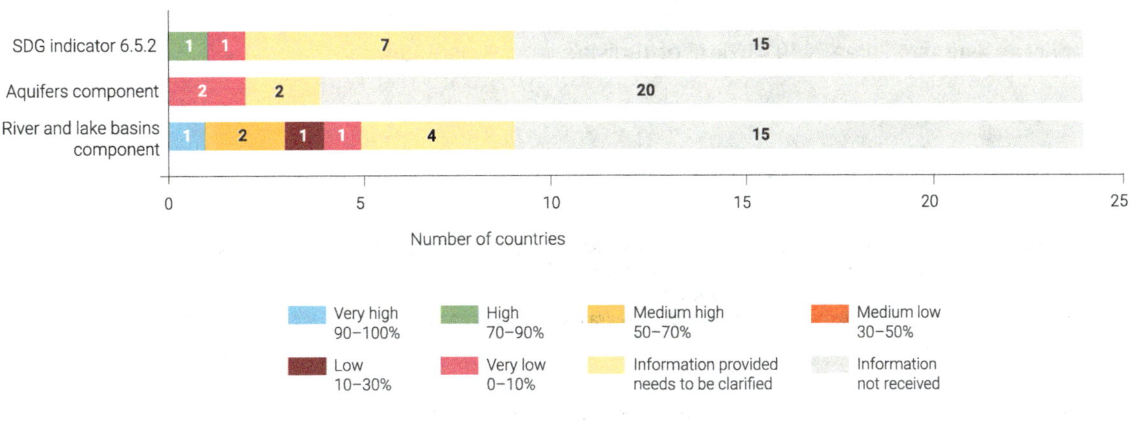

3.2.2. Northern Africa

and Western Asia

Out of 23 countries in Northern Africa and Western Asia, 21 share transboundary basins. Responses were received from 12 of these 21 countries, and the overall indicator value is available for seven countries (Armenia, Georgia, Iraq, Jordan, Morocco, Qatar and Tunisia).

Based on the seven countries where data are available, the overall indicator value is 17 per cent. Tunisia has operational arrangements for 81 per cent of its transboundary basin area, whereas the other six countries have less than 30 per cent of their transboundary basin area covered. Four of the six countries have no operational arrangements in place.

For river and lake basins, the average national proportion of transboundary basin area covered by an operational arrangement for water cooperation is 11 per cent, compared with 16 per cent for transboundary aquifers. This is a specific feature of this region in which, contrary to other parts of the world, cooperation on transboundary aquifers has advanced more than cooperation on surface water.

Indeed, water availability from river and lake basins tends to be intermittent at best, due to the arid to semi-arid climate found in much of Northern Africa and Western Asia. In these areas, groundwater plays a major role in terms of water availability. This is particularly evident in Northern Africa, where two major transboundary aquifers dominate the water landscape, namely the North-Western Sahara Aquifer System (NWSAS, shared between Algeria, Libya and Tunisia) and the Nubian Sandstone Aquifer System (NSAS, shared between Chad, Egypt, Libya and Sudan). The importance placed upon aquifers in these countries is illustrated by the SDG indicator 6.5.2 report from Tunisia, where the NWSAS covering an estimated 80,000 km² of the country is considered operational. In contrast, only an estimated area of 19,416 km² of Tunisia's

territory is covered by five river basins, none of which are currently considered to be covered by an operational arrangement for cooperation. While relatively less important, these basins nevertheless represent an important resource for local populations.

Arrangements for cooperation are in place for both the NWSAS and the NSAS. In 2002, Algeria, Libya and Tunisia entered into an agreement to establish a consultation mechanism for the NWSAS "to coordinate, promote and facilitate the rational management of the NWSAS water resources".[52] Since its adoption, this mechanism has conducted joint studies to better understand the aquifer system, developed "operational recommendations for sustainable water resources management of the North-Western Sahara Aquifer System", with a particular focus on sustainable irrigation systems, and sought to strengthen legal and institutional frameworks.[53]

Cooperation concerning the NSAS was initiated by Egypt and Libya in the early 1970s, and formalized with the creation of the Joint Authority for the Management of the NSAS in 1992. Sudan subsequently became a member in 1992, followed by Chad in 1999.[54] Cooperation through the Joint Authority has improved knowledge and understanding of NSAS, and led to the four countries' adoption of a Strategic Action Programme in 2012.[55] This programme aims to address the key transboundary concerns collectively identified by Chad, Egypt, Libya and Sudan, including declining water levels related to abstractions; damage or loss of the ecosystem and biodiversity of the oasis that are linked to the aquifer; and water quality deterioration from agricultural, industrial and urban pollution.[56]

Evidence of transboundary water cooperation on aquifers can also be found in the 2015 agreement on the Al-Disi/Saq-Ram Aquifer shared between Jordan and Saudi Arabia.[57] This agreement aims to ensure the "proper management, utilization and sustainability" of the aquifer waters, and establishes a joint technical committee to oversee the agreement's implementation.[58]

---

[52] Establishment of a Consultation Mechanism for the Northwestern Sahara Aquifer System, 19 and 20 December 2002, in Stefano Burchi and Kerstin Mechlem, *Groundwater in international law – compilation of treaties and other legal instruments* (FAO and UNESCO 2005).

[53] See http://sass.oss-online.org/en/sass-project (accessed 2 July 2018).

[54] International Atomic Agency, *Regional Strategic Action Programme for the Nubian Sandstone Aquifer System – Final Report*, https://iaea.org/sites/default/files/sap180913.pdf (accessed 2 July 2018), pp. 15-18.

[55] *Id.*

[56] *Id.*, p. 9.

[57] Agreement between the Government of the Hashemite Kingdom of Jordan and the Government of the Kingdom of Saudi Arabia for the Management and Utilization of the Ground Waters in the Al-Sag/Al-Disi Layer, 30 April 2015, https://internationalwaterlaw.org/documents/regionaldocs/Disi_Aquifer_Agreement-English2015.pdf (accessed 2 July 2018).

[58] *Id.*, articles 2 and 3.

Figure 12: Northern Africa and Western Asia: national level of cooperation on transboundary water, river and lake basins, and aquifers, and countries where further clarification is still needed

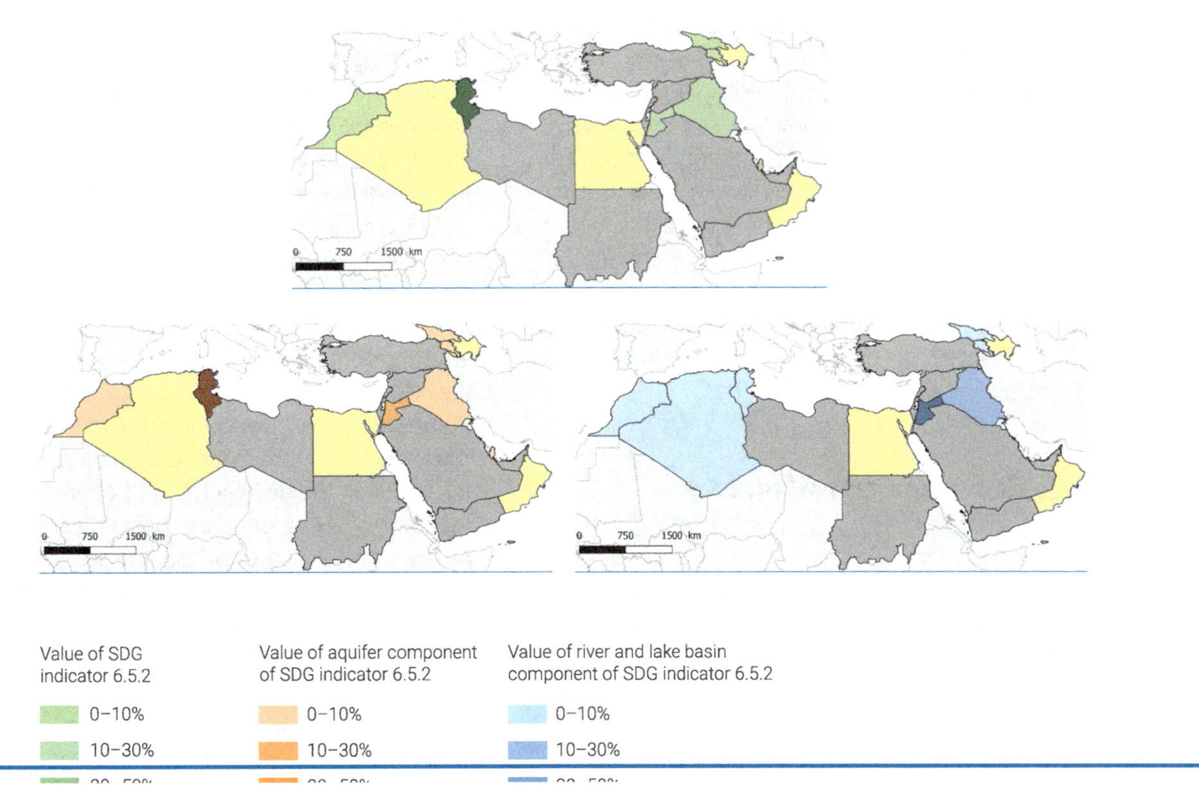

Figure 13: Northern Africa and Western Asia: breakdown of the number of countries sharing waters and level of cooperation on transboundary water for SDG indicator 6.5.2, aquifers, and river and lake basins

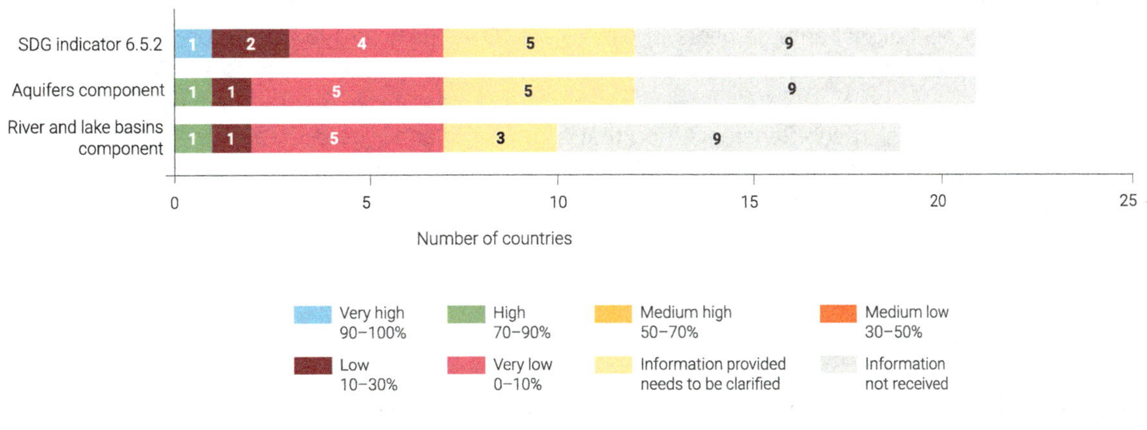

While transboundary aquifers dominate the water landscape in much of Northern Africa and Western Asia, cooperation concerning several major river basins is also critical to the pursuit of sustainable development in the region. For example, basin-wide operational arrangements are currently lacking in the Tigris-Euphrates River Basin (shared between Iraq, Syria and Turkey) and the Jordan River Basin (shared between Israel, Jordan, State of Palestine and Syria), although there are significant signs of cooperation. Jordan, for instance, reports that its bilateral arrangement with Israel is operational and also recognizes the role of the joint water committee in implementing the arrangement.[59] Meanwhile, Georgia reported cooperative activities in the Kura-Araks River Basin, which is shared between Armenia, Azerbaijan, Georgia, Iran and Turkey. However, there is no arrangement for cooperation at the basin level. Azerbaijan and Georgia are currently negotiating a bilateral cooperation agreement for the protection and sustainable use of the Kura River Basin water resources.

3.2.3. Sub-Saharan Africa

Out of 48 countries in sub-Saharan Africa, 42 share transboundary basins.[60] Reports were received from 33 of these 42 countries. While 13 reports still require clarification, the overall indicator value can be calculated for 20 countries.

Based on the 20 countries where national data are available, the overall indicator value is 57 per cent. Among these countries, half have operational arrangements in place for over 70 per cent of their transboundary basins, and only two countries (Botswana and Namibia) have operational arrangements in place for all their transboundary basins. Three countries report having no operational arrangements in place for any of their transboundary basins.

Out of the 27 countries in sub-Saharan Africa that reported a value for river and lake basins, 10 countries report having operational arrangements in place for all

their transboundary river and lake basins. In terms of aquifers, six countries report that operational arrangements are in place for more than 70 per cent of their transboundary aquifers, and nine countries report that less than 30 per cent of their transboundary aquifers are covered by operational arrangements. Eight of these nine countries report that no operational arrangements are in place.

Relatively high levels of operational arrangements concerning transboundary river and lake basins can be found in Central, West and Southern Africa. Data are available for eight of the 12 countries in the Southern Africa Development Community (SADC) region that share transboundary river and lake basins. These eight countries (Angola, Botswana, Democratic Republic of Congo, Lesotho, Namibia, South Africa, Zambia and Zimbabwe) report that over 70 per cent of their transboundary river and lake basins are covered by operational arrangements. The adoption of the Revised Protocol on Shared Watercourses in the Southern African Development Community (Revised SADC Protocol) in 2000 constituted an important milestone in the development of operational arrangements for transboundary basins across Southern Africa.[61] As a framework instrument, which closely mirrors the Watercourses Convention, the Revised SADC Protocol has proven to be an effective tool for fostering cooperation at the regional level.

In Central Africa, several countries recognize the importance of the International Commission of the Congo-Oubangui-Sangha Basin (CICOS) in shifting cooperation on the basin from focusing on navigation to broader IWRM activities.[62] Significant developments are also evident in the Lake Chad Basin (shared between Cameroon, Central African Republic, Chad, Niger and Nigeria) through the adoption of the Convention and Statute of the Commission of the Lake Chad Basin in 1964, and more recently with the adoption of the Lake Chad Basin Water Charter in 2012 by Cameroon, Central African Republic, Chad, Libya, Niger and Nigeria.[63] These efforts are all underpinned by the 2009 Regional Water Policy of the Economic Community of Central African States.[64]

---

[59] Article 6 and Annex II, Treaty of Peace between the State of Israel and the Hashemite Kingdom of Jordan, 26 October 1994, https://peacemaker.un.org/sites/peacemaker.un.org/files/IL%20JO_941026_PeaceTreatyIsraelJordan.pdf (accessed 2 July 2018).

[60] UNEP-DHI and UNEP (n 14).

[61] Revised Protocol on Shared Watercourses in the Southern African Development Community, 7 August 2000, http://sadc.int/files/3413/6698/6218/Revised_Protocol_on_Shared_Watercourses_-_2000_-_English.pdf (accessed 2 July 2018).

[62] Accord establishing a uniform river regime and creating CICOS, 21 November 1999, https://iea.uoregon.edu/treaty-text/1999-congooubanguisanghacommissionfrtxt (accessed 2 July 2018).

[63] Water Charter of the Lake Chad Basin, 8 April 2011, https://africanwaterfacility.org/fileadmin/uploads/awf/Projects/MULTIN-LAKECHAD-Water-Charter.pdf (accessed 2 July 2018).

[64] See http://cmsdata.iucn.org/downloads/politique_des_ressources_en_eau_de_lafrique_de_louest.pdf (accessed 3 July 2018).

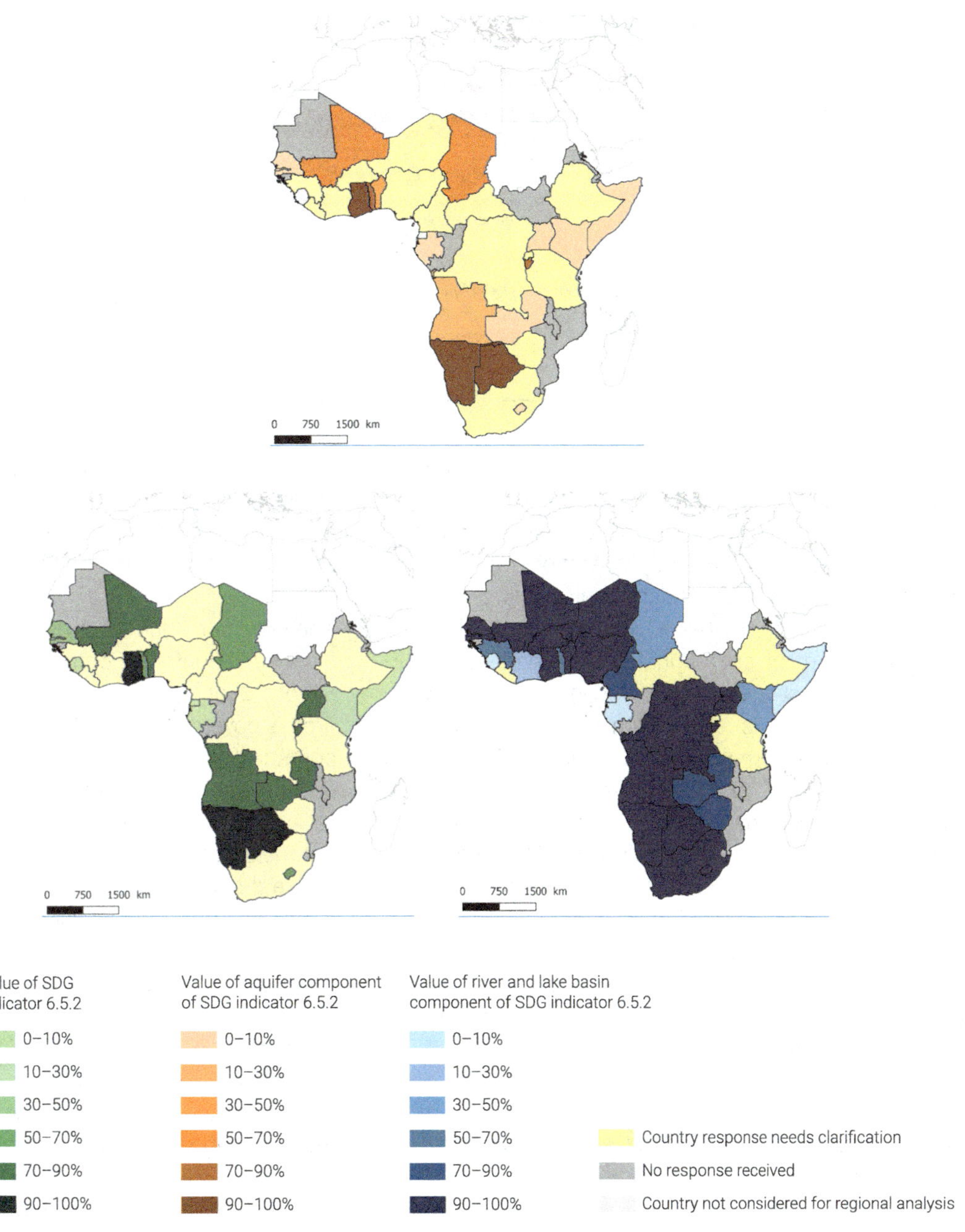

Most countries in West Africa also record high levels of operational arrangements for their transboundary river and lake basins. Basin-wide legal frameworks, supported by joint bodies, are in place for the major river basins within the region, including the Senegal, Gambia, Volta and Niger rivers.

While responses from countries in West Africa are limited, evidence of transboundary water cooperation is found within the responses concerning the Nile, which is the region's most significant transboundary river basin. Several countries noted the key role that the Nile Basin Initiative has played in fostering cooperation since its adoption in 1999, although the challenges associated with the establishment of the Nile Basin Commission and entry into force of the Nile River Basin Cooperative Framework Agreement were also recognized. [65]

[65] Agreement on the Nile River Basin Cooperative Framework, 22 May 2009, http://nilebasin.org/images/docs/CFA%20-%20English%20%20FrenchVersion.pdf (accessed 2 July 2018).

Figure 15: Sub-Saharan Africa: breakdown of the number of countries sharing waters and level of cooperation on transboundary water for SDG indicator 6.5.2, aquifers, and river and lake basins

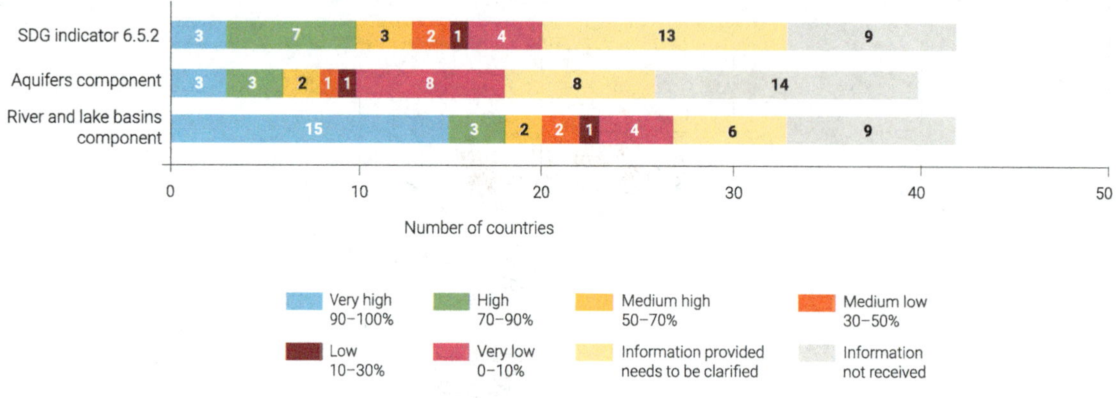

Increasing reliable water supplies throughout Africa will depend on groundwater, especially in times of drought, and in the semi-arid northern and southern parts of the region.[66] Currently, operational arrangements related to transboundary aquifers across the region are limited. Of the 10 countries that identified some form of operational arrangement related to aquifers, most are included within river and lake basins arrangements, apart from the Nubian Sandstone Aquifer System (as discussed above). Through the Integrated and Joint Water Resources Management of the Iullemeden, Taoudeni-Tanezrouft Aquifer Systems and the Niger River (GICRESAIT) project, Algeria, Benin, Burkina Faso, Mali, Mauritania, Niger and Nigeria are seeking to strengthen transboundary cooperation on their shared aquifer systems.[67] The case of the Stampriet, as discussed above, also illustrates the growing importance of cooperation over transboundary aquifers within the region.

3.2.4. Europe and Northern America

Of the 45 countries in Europe and Northern America, 43 share transboundary rivers, lakes and aquifers. Responses were received from 40 of these 43 countries, and an overall indicator value of 88 per cent is available for 24 countries. Fifteen countries report having all their transboundary basins covered by operational arrangements.

The indicator value for river and lake basins is available for 34 countries. For these countries, an estimated 81 per cent of transboundary river and lake basin area is covered by operational arrangements. Twenty countries have all their transboundary river and lake basin area covered by operational arrangements.

For the 24 countries in Europe and Northern America where the indicator value for transboundary aquifers is available, the average value is 82 per cent.

High levels of operational arrangements throughout Europe and Northern America reflect a long tradition of cooperation across the region. For example, one of the key legal frameworks for cooperation between Canada and the United States – which established the International Joint Commission between both countries – dates from 1909.[68] Canada and the United States have supplemented this bilateral arrangement through the adoption of several instruments relating to the Lake of the Woods,[69] the Niagara River,[70] the Columbia River,[71] and the Great Lakes.[72]

[66] Alan M. MacDonald *et al.* 2012. Quantitative maps of groundwater resources in Africa. *Environmental Research Letters*, Vol. 7, No. 2, pp. 1-7.

[67] Sahara and Sahel Observatory, GICRESAIT, http://oss-online.org/en/integrated-water-resources-management-iullemeden-taoudeni-tanezrouft-aquifer-systems-niger-river (accessed 2 July 2018).

[68] Treaty Between the United States and Great Britain Relating to Boundary Waters, and Questions Arising Between the United States and Canada, 11 January 1909, http://ijc.org/en_/BWT (accessed 2 July 2018).

[69] Convention and Protocol Regulating the Level of the Lake of the Woods, and of Identical Letters of Reference Submitting to the International Joint Commission certain Questions as to the Regulation of the Levels of Rainy Lake and other Upper Waters, 24 February 1925, http://ijc.org/files/dockets/Docket%203/Docket%203%20Convention%20and%20Protocol.pdf (accessed 2 July 2018).

[70] Treaty Between the United States of America and Canada Relating to the Uses of the Waters of the Niagara River, 27 February 1950, https://internationalwaterlaw.org/documents/regionaldocs/niagra1950.html (accessed 2 July 2018).

[71] Treaty between Canada and the United States of America relating to Cooperative Development of the Water Resources of the Columbia River Basin, 16 September 1964, https://crt2014-2024review.gov/Files/International%20Documents%20ColumbiaRiverTreaty.pdf (accessed 2 July 2018).

[72] Protocol Amending the Agreement between Canada and the United States of America on Great Lakes Water Quality, 1978, as Amended on 16 October 1983, and on 18 November 1987. Signed 7 September 2012, https://binational.net//wp-content/uploads/2014/05/1094_Canada-USA-GLWQA-_e.pdf (accessed 2 July 2018).

Figure 16: Europe and Northern America: national level of cooperation on transboundary water, river and lake basins, and aquifers, and countries where further clarification is still needed

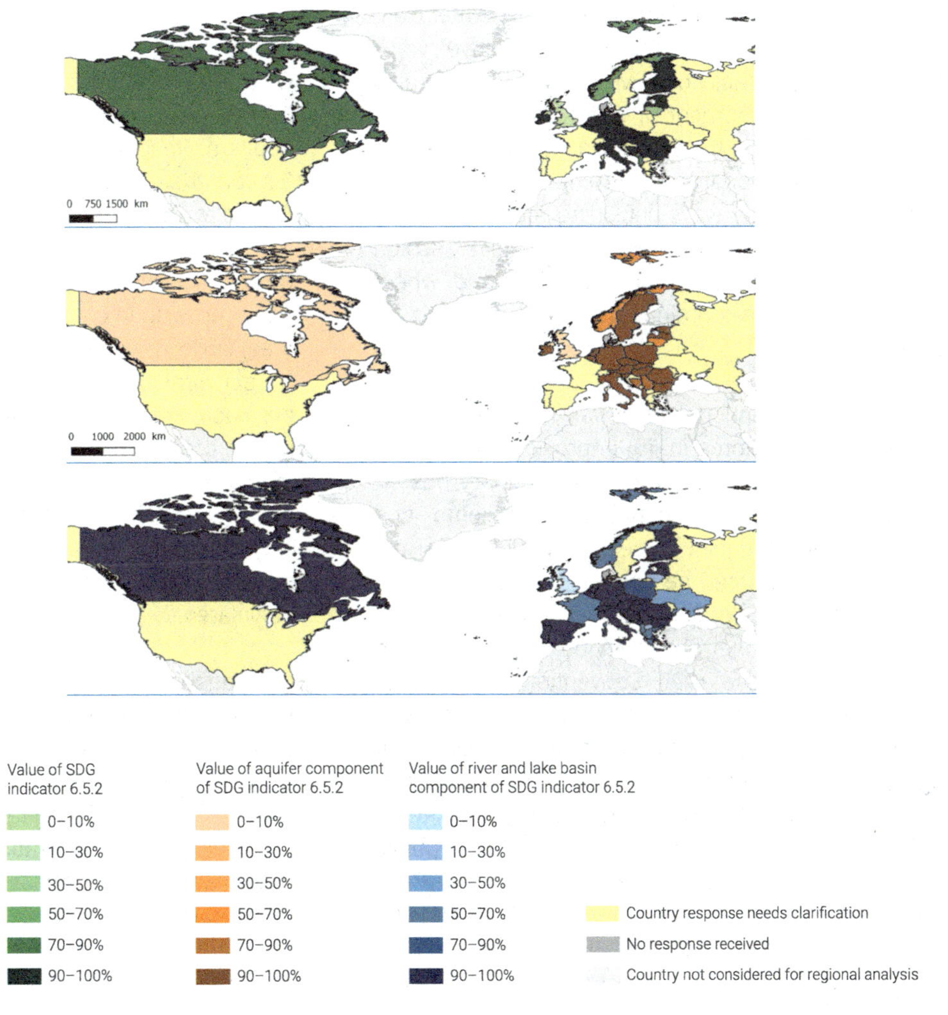

Figure 17: Europe and Northern America: breakdown of the number of countries sharing waters and level of cooperation on transboundary water for SDG indicator 6.5.2, aquifers, and river and lake basins

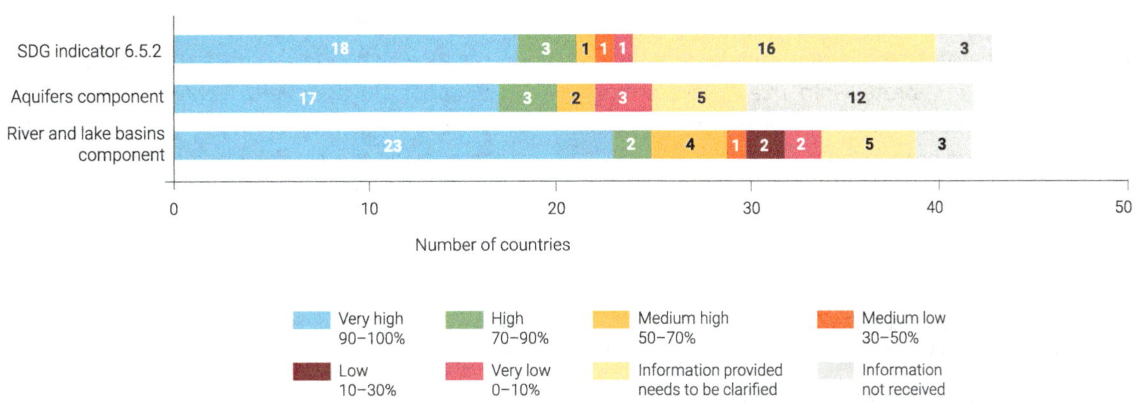

Across Europe, cooperation at the basin and bilateral levels has been strengthened, and at times triggered, by the development of two key regional instruments: the EU Water Framework Directive and the Water Convention. The EU Water Framework Directive, while only directly applicable to EU Member States, has also inspired the development of water law and policy in countries bordering the EU region. The Directive has influenced operational arrangements for transboundary basins in many ways, including requiring States to designate international river basin districts, assign appropriate authorities to those districts, and, where possible, develop a coordinated management plan for each district.

The Water Convention, which was adopted in 1992 and entered into force in 1996, provides more specific commitments related to transboundary basins, including the establishment of agreements and arrangements, and joint bodies. The influence of the Water Convention can be seen in the adoption and implementation of major basin agreements across Europe, such as the 1994 Danube River Protection Convention and the 1999 Convention for the Protection of the Rhine. The Water Convention has also proven to be an important basis for the negotiation of agreements in newly independent States within Eastern and Southern Europe, the Caucasus and Central Asia – such as the agreement between the Republic of Moldova and Ukraine related to the Dniester River Basin, which entered into force in 2017;[73] and the Memorandum of Understanding for the Management of the Extended Transboundary Drin Basin, which was adopted in 2011.[74]

In terms of transboundary aquifers, approaches differ between Europe and Northern America. In Northern America, the 1909 Boundary Waters Treaty does not reference groundwater, and none of the 10 transboundary aquifers that Canada and the United States share are considered to have operational arrangements in place. In contrast, 21 countries in Europe identify operational arrangements in the transboundary aquifers that they share with their neighbours, all of which are incorporated into river basin arrangements that promote the integrated management of surface water and groundwater.

3.2.5. Latin America and the Caribbean

Of the 33 countries in Latin America and the Caribbean, 22 share transboundary rivers, lakes and aquifers. Responses were received from 13 of these 22 countries, and an overall indicator value of 24 per cent is available for nine countries.

Of these nine countries, only Ecuador has operational arrangements in place for all its transboundary basin area, while such arrangements cover 67 per cent and 51 per cent of Brazil's and Paraguay's transboundary basins respectively. Most of the other countries have either no or very few operational arrangements in place. For instance, Venezuela has operational arrangements in place for 4 per cent of its transboundary basin area, and Mexico has operational arrangements in place for 1 per cent of its transboundary basin area.

For transboundary river and lake basins, three countries report that at least 70 per cent of their transboundary basin area is covered by operational arrangements, namely Brazil (98 per cent), Ecuador (100 per cent) and Paraguay (100 per cent). Only Ecuador reports to have operational arrangements in place for all its transboundary aquifers; the other nine countries record no operational arrangements.

Despite the overall indicator value for Latin America and the Caribbean being relatively low (24 per cent), efforts to foster cooperation over transboundary waters exist across the region. In this region of primarily tropical and temperate areas, much of the focus of these cooperative efforts has been on river and lake basins. Ninety-two per cent of the total transboundary river basin area of the region, and 68 per cent of its total available freshwater, is contained in three river basins: Amazon, La Plata and Orinoco.[75] In 1978, an arrangement for the Amazon was adopted by all eight countries sharing the basin (Bolivia, Brazil, Columbia, Ecuador, Guyana, Peru, Surinam and Venezuela).[76] An important step in supporting implementation of the treaty was the establishment of the Amazon Cooperation Treaty Organization in 1998.[77] Since 1969, the La

---

[73] Treaty between the Government of the Republic of Moldova and the Cabinet of Ministers of Ukraine on Co-operation in the Field of Protection and Sustainable Development of the Dniester River Basin, 29 November 2012, https://unece.org/fileadmin/DAM/env/water/activities/Dniester/Dniester-treaty-final-EN-29Nov2012_web.pdf (accessed 2 July 2018).

[74] Memorandum of Understanding for the Management of the Extended Transboundary Drin Basin, 12 November 2011, http://unece.org/fileadmin/DAM/env/water/South-Estern_Europe_Drin/MOU_Drin_Strategic_Shared_vision_Final.pdf (accessed 2 July 2018).

[75] UNEP et al. 2007. *Hydropolitical Vulnerability and Resilience along International Waters – Latin America and the Caribbean*, p. 50.

[76] *Id.* p. 59.

[77] ACTO/PS, *Legal Basis of the Amazon Cooperation Treaty – Updated summary 2003-2012* (ACTO 2013).

Figure 18: Latin America and the Caribbean: national level of cooperation on transboundary water, river and lake basins, and aquifers, and countries where further clarification is still needed

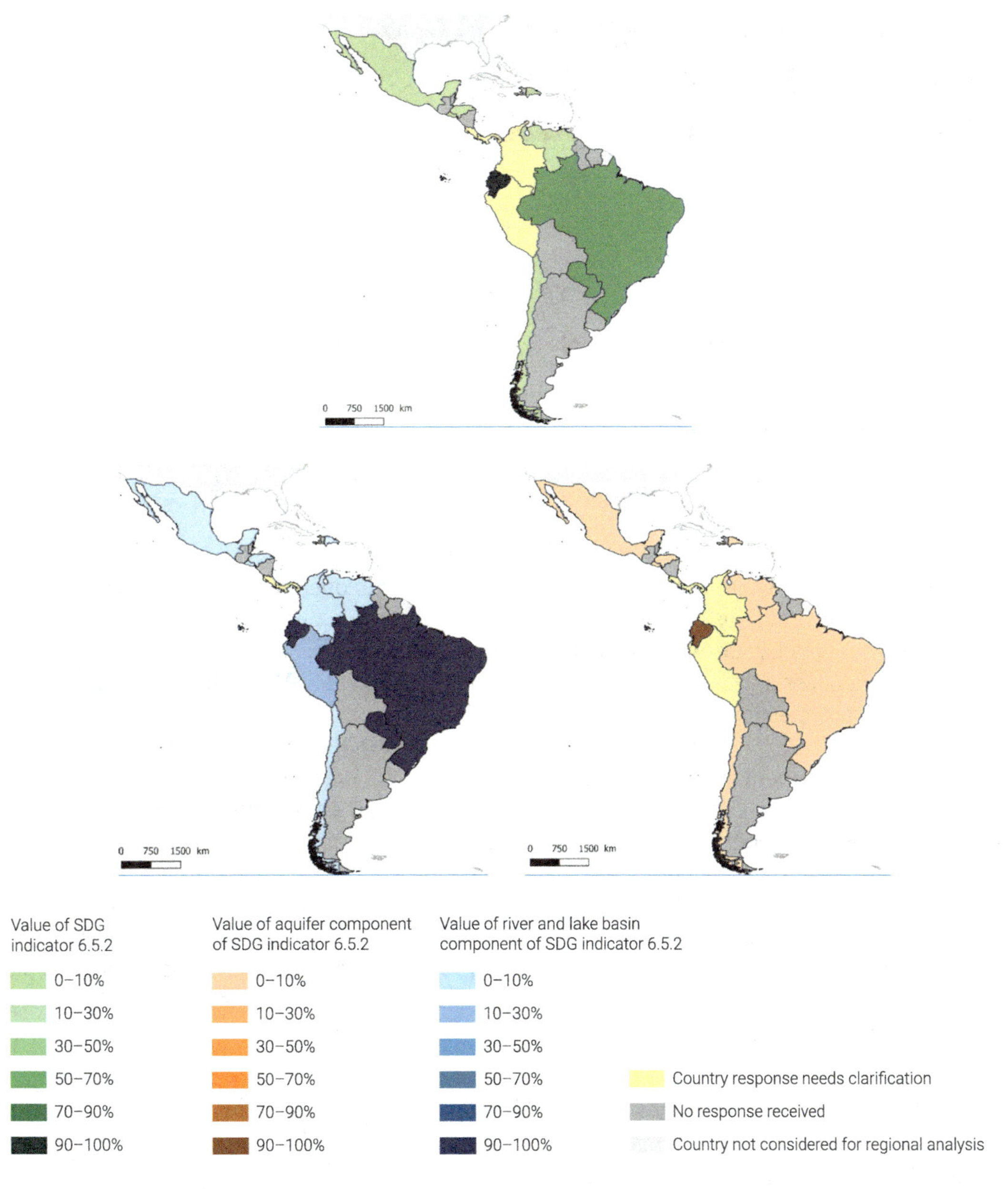

Plata Basin has also been covered by a treaty framework, which aims to promote "the harmonious development and physical integration of the River Plate Basin and its zones of direct and measurable influence".[78] Implementation of the treaty is supported by the Intergovernmental Coordinating Committee of the La Plata Basin Countries (CIC), and numerous sub-basin legal and institutional arrangements, such as those for the Itaipu Binational Commission (see above).[79] No cooperative arrangements covering the third largest river basin in the region, the Orinoco, are in place.

Eight countries in Central America share transboundary basins, many of which – as illustrated in the reports of El Salvador and Honduras – do not have operational arrangements. However, there are efforts to foster cooperation, including on the Sixaola River between Costa Rica and Panama, where a binational

---

[78] Art. 1, Treaty of the River Pate Basin, 23 April 1969, https://internationalwaterlaw.org/documents/regionaldocs/La_Plata-1969.pdf (accessed 2 July 2018).
[79] World Water Assessment Programme, La Plata Basin Case Study: Final Report, http://unesdoc.unesco.org/images/0015/001512/151252e.pdf (accessed 2 July 2018).

Figure 19: Latin America and the Caribbean: breakdown of the number of countries sharing waters and level of cooperation on transboundary water for SDG indicator 6.5.2, aquifers, and river and lake basins

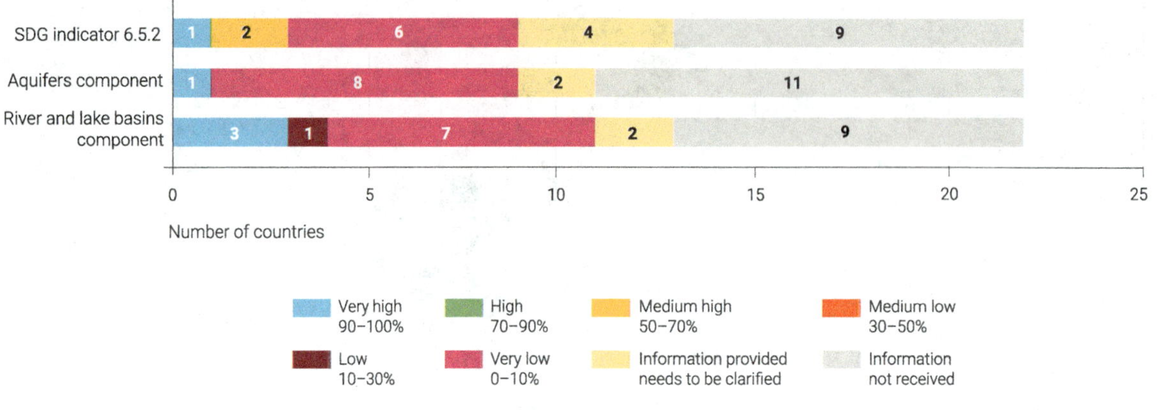

commission was established in 2007.[80] Additionally, in some instances, such as the Treaty between El Salvador, Guatemala and Honduras for the Execution of the Trifinio Plan, cooperation on water-related activities has taken place under a wider arrangement focused on environmental protection.[81]

Other efforts to strengthen cooperation on transboundary aquifers in the Latin American and Caribbean region include the adoption of the Guarani Aquifer Agreement between Argentina, Brazil, Paraguay and Uruguay in 2012. A major milestone was reached in April 2018, when Paraguay became the last of the four countries to ratify the Agreement.[82] Covering 1.2 million km², the Guarani Aquifer is estimated to be the second largest aquifer system in the world.[83]

3.3. Thematic analysis – exploring operationality

Having considered SDG indicator 6.5.2 results at both the global and regional levels, this section explores the results of the first reporting exercise from the perspective of the four operationality criteria. In addition, an analysis of the arrangements that do not satisfy all four operationality criteria is provided.

3.3.1. Arrangements for cooperation falling short of the operationality criteria

By disaggregating the national data on SDG indicator 6.5.2 by the four individual criteria, it is possible to assess non-operational arrangements, and ask which criterion or criteria precludes those arrangements from becoming operational.

Of the 107 responses that were submitted by countries sharing transboundary basins, 36 arrangements were listed as not being operational. Twenty-two of these 36 arrangements cover basins or sub-basins that are also covered by operational arrangements. For example, the 1992 Agreement between Namibia and South Africa establishing a Permanent Water Commission relating to the Lower Orange River is not considered operational because no joint or coordinated management plan or joint objectives are in place. However, a basin-wide operational arrangement – the 2000 Agreement for the Establishment of

[80] See IUCN, 'The Binational Commission of the Sixaola River Basin opens path for its sustainability through teamwork', https://iucn.org/news/mexico-central-america-and-caribbean/201702/binational-commission-sixaola-river-basin-opens-path-its-sustainability-through-teamwork (accessed 2 July 2018).
[81] IGRAC (n 28).
[82] Pursuant to Article 21, the Agreement will enter into force on the 30th day after Paraguay deposits its instrument of ratification with Brazil.
[83] IGRAC (n 28).

the Orange-Senqu Commission – covers the entire Orange-Senqu Basin. Transforming these 22 arrangements into operational arrangements, while beneficial insofar as supporting the joint sustainable management of shared resources, would not have an impact on the SDG 6.5.2 indicator value.

Given that it is only possible to analyse 14 non-operational arrangements, the significance of this analysis is limited. While the SDG indicator 6.5.2 methodology requests that countries include *all* their transboundary basin arrangements within the reporting template, there may have been a tendency for countries to include only arrangements considered operational. Similarly, data are only available for the 107 countries that responded to the request to report. Data on non-operational arrangements might therefore be enhanced in future reporting exercises.

3.3.2. Diverse arrangements for transboundary water cooperation

Formal arrangements offer an important means by which to foster cooperation between countries over transboundary waters. Such instruments reflect a formal commitment by countries that can offer the basis for a long-term, predictable and resilient framework for cooperation. The Water Convention (article 3), the Watercourses Convention (article 9) and the Draft Articles on the Law of Transboundary Aquifers (article 9) all recognize the importance of having an arrangement in place for a particular river, lake or aquifer, or part thereof.

SDG indicator 6.5.2 reports suggest that countries have entered into very diverse arrangements. An overview of the different types of arrangements listed in the national reports for 6.5.2, together with examples, is provided in Figure 21. This overview suggests that there is no "one size fits all" when it comes to adopting an arrangement, but that countries tailor them to the particular historical, legal and political context in which they are working. These basin-specific arrangements are also supported by arrangements adopted at the regional and global (multi-basin) levels, such as the Water Convention, the Watercourses Convention, the EU Water Framework Directive and the Revised

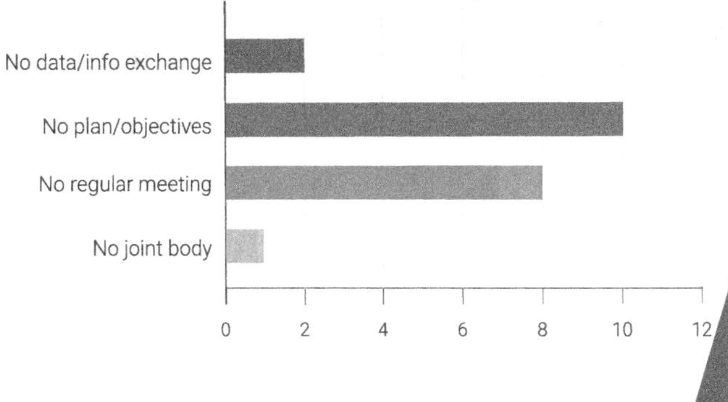

Figure 20: Operationality criteria not fulfilled

SADC Protocol; as well as other multilateral arrangements addressing water-related issues such as biodiversity, climate change, wetlands, human rights and foreign investment.[84]

A further area of diversity concerns the Parties to a particular agreement or arrangement. While most agreements and arrangements are concluded at the national level by countries, subnational entities and non-State entities may also become party to them. For example, in addition to Belgium, France and the Netherlands, the Belgian regions of Walloon, Flemish and Brussels-Capital are also Parties to the 2002 Agreement on the River Scheldt. Along similar lines, the 2007 Arrangement on the Protection and Recharge of the Franco-Swiss Genevois Aquifer was concluded between the Republic and Canton of Geneva on the one part, and the Community of the Annemassienne Region, the Community of the Genevois Rural Districts, and the Rural District of Viry on the other.[85]

The first reporting exercise has also illustrated differing approaches relating to the functional scope of arrangements. A common approach has been for two countries to enter into bilateral treaties that cover all their transboundary waters.

---

84 See for example Convention on Biological Diversity, 5 June 1992, https://cbd.int/convention/text/ (accessed 2 July 2018); and United Nations Framework Convention on Climate Change, 9 May 1992, https://unfccc.int/resource/docs/convkp/conveng.pdf (accessed 2 July 2018).
85 Gabriel de los Cobos. 2010. 'The Transboundary Aquifer of the Geneva Region (Switzerland and France): Successfully Managed for 30 years by the State of Geneva and France', International Conference on Transboundary Aquifers: challenges and new directives'. Paris, http://siagua.org/sites/default/files/documentos/documentos/geneva.pdf (accessed 2 July 2018).

Figure 21: Table summarizing the different types of transboundary basin arrangements

Type of instrument	Characteristics	Examples
Framework convention	Framework conventions tend to set out the main substantive and procedural rules and principles for governing a particular river, lake or aquifer system. This type of agreement also tends to establish joint institutional arrangements, such as a River Basin Commission.	**2010** Guarani Aquifer Agreement **1970** Treaty on the Rio de la Plata Basin **1995** Agreement on the Cooperation for the Sustainable Development of the Mekong River Basin **1994** Convention on Cooperation for the Protection and Sustainable Use of the Danube River **1998** Convention on the Protection of the Rhine **2000** Agreement for the Establishment of the Orange-Senqu Commission **2003** Convention on the Sustainable Management of Lake Tanganyika
Bilateral treaty	Countries sharing several transboundary waters tend to adopt bilateral treaties. These treaties tend to set out general rules and principles covering all transboundary waters, and may establish joint institutional arrangements such as intergovernmental commissions or working groups. By covering all transboundary waters, groundwater is indirectly included.	**2017** Agreement between Uzbekistan and Turkmenistan on Cooperation in the Field of Water Management **2017** Agreement between Poland and the Czech Republic on Cooperation on Transboundary Rivers in the Field of Water Management **1990** Agreement between Botswana and Namibia on the Establishment of a Joint Water Commission
Protocols	Protocols tend to be concluded on the basis of more general founding agreements.	**2012** Great Lakes Water Quality Protocol **2003** Protocol for Sustainable Development of Lake Victoria Basin
Memorandum of Understanding (MoU)	MoUs tend to include broader principles of cooperation and are often adopted at the interministerial level. MoUs may or may not be legally binding.	**2011** MoU for the Management of the Extended Transboundary Drin Basin **2015** MoU between Kenya and Tanzania for Joint Water Resources Management of the Transboundary Mara River Basin
Joint Declaration	Joint declarations may cover one basin or several basins. Declarations tend to include broader principles of cooperation and are often adopted at the interministerial, rather than interstate, level. Joint declarations may or may not be legally binding.	**2010** Joint Declaration on Understanding and Cooperation in the Field of Use of Water Resources on the Respective Territories of the Shared River Basins between Bulgaria and Greece
Exchange of Letters	Exchanges of letters tend to set out specific commitments that may have been agreed at a particular meeting, or reflect an update of an existing agreement or arrangement.	**2002 & 2009** Exchange of letters between the Ministers of Germany, the Netherlands, Lower-Saxony, and Nordrhein-Westfalen (implementing the EU Water Framework Directive and the Floods Directive)
Minutes	Minutes tend to be records of commitments agreed at a particular meeting. They may assist in the interpretation of a treaty arrangement.	**1980** Minutes of the Joint Iraqi-Turkish Committee for Economic and Technical Cooperation **1922-2017** International Boundary and Water Commission between US and Mexico has adopted 323 Minutes **2002** Minutes adopted by Algeria, Libya and Tunisia on the North-Western Sahara Aquifer System through the establishment of a Consultation Mechanism

Another well-used approach has been for countries to conclude agreements for specific transboundary rivers, lakes and aquifers. Most of these agreements cover rivers, with a small number focused on specific lakes or aquifers. Other arrangements might cover part of a basin, such as a tributary or lagoon – for example, the 1977 Treaty on Cooperation for the Utilization of the Natural Resources and the Development of the Mirim Lagoon Basin, or the 2002 Framework Agreement on the Sava River Basin adopted by Bosnia and Herzegovina, Croatia, Slovakia and the Federal Republic of Yugoslavia, which covers a sub-basin of the Danube River Basin.[86] A further approach has been to embed transboundary water arrangements into wider cooperation treaties, such as peace treaties (see the 1994 Israel-Jordan Peace Treaty) or treaties covering border regions (see the 1987 Agreement between Guatemala and Mexico on the Protection and Improvement of the Environment in the Border Area).

SDG indicator 6.5.2 national reports also show significant diversity in the topics that are covered. Whereas some arrangements focus on specific infrastructure projects or carrying out a joint study, others focus on certain uses, such as fisheries, water allocation, water supply, monitoring, flood control, water quality and pollution, hydropower or irrigation. More recently, arrangements have tended to take a holistic approach, in the hope of fostering sustainable development at the basin level. For example, the Treaty between Ukraine and Moldova on Cooperation in the Field of Protection and Sustainable Development of the Dniester River Basin entered into force in 2017. The holistic nature of this basin-wide instrument is reflected in its objective, which includes, "achieving rational and environmentally sound use and protection of water and other natural resources and ecosystems of the Dniester River Basin".[87] Based on the SDG indicator 6.5.2 national reports, Figure 22 provides an overview of the sectoral scope of arrangements. This figure clearly shows that the majority of agreements and arrangements that have been included in the reports adopt a multi-sector approach.

The arrangements do not tend to be static instruments, with those that establish joint bodies having proven to be particularly adept at evolving in response to the needs and interests of the Parties concerned. For example, the International Boundary & Water Commission between Mexico and the United States has adopted over 320 "minutes" that seek to support the development and implementation of the 1944 Treaty on the Utilization of Waters of the Colorado and Tijuana Rivers and of the Rio Grande. Minutes cover a range of issues, including cross-border sanitation, water conveyance during droughts, the construction of dams, water salinity, and environmental flows.[88] Once approved, the minutes are considered binding upon both Parties.[89] In other instances, countries have demonstrated their preference for revising older arrangements. For example, in 2010 Finland and Sweden replaced a bilateral arrangement that they had entered into in 1971 with a new arrangement. The new arrangement was designed to better reflect legal instruments that had subsequently been developed at the regional level, including the Water Convention and the EU Water Framework Directive.

Figure 22: SDG 6.5.2 national reports – responses to the question: what is the sectoral scope of the agreement or arrangement?

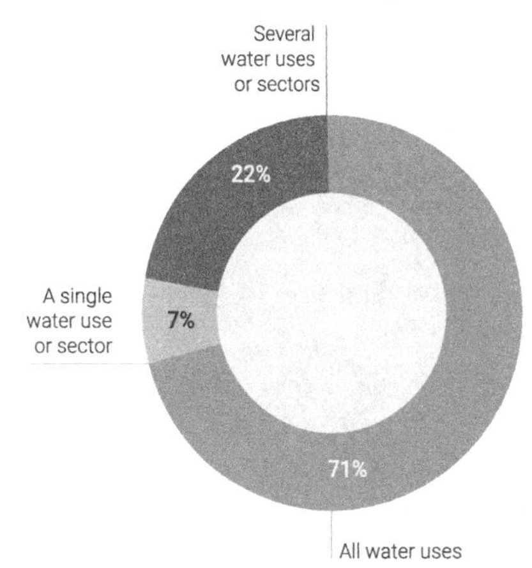

---

[86] Serbia replaced the Federal Republic of Yugoslavia as a Party to the Sava River Basin legal framework.

[87] Treaty between the Government of the Republic of Moldova and the Cabinet of Ministers of Ukraine on Cooperation in the Field of Protection and Sustainable Development of the Dniester River Basin, 29 November 2012, https://unece.org/fileadmin/DAM/env/water/activities/Dniester/Dniester-treaty-final-EN-29Nov2012_web.pdf (accessed 2 July 2018).

[88] See generally, Nicole T. Carter et al., US-Mexican Water Sharing: Background and Recent Developments, https://fas.org/sgp/crs/row/R43312.pdf (accessed 2 July 2018).

[89] See Art. 25, Treaty Between the US and Mexico on the Utilization of Waters of the Colorado and Tijuana Rivers and of the Rio Grande, 3 February 1944, https://ibwc.gov/Files/1944Treaty.pdf (accessed 2 July 2018).

3.3.3. The importance of joint bodies in sustaining cooperation

Establishing some form of institutional coordination is critical to ensuring that the arrangements for transboundary water cooperation are implemented effectively.[90] Joint bodies have proven to be an important means by which countries foster cooperation through, for example, regular communication, exchange of data and information, the development of joint plans and projects, the engagement of stakeholders in transboundary water management, and the resolution or avoidance of disputes.[91]

The importance of such arrangements is reflected in the Watercourses Convention, wherein countries are encouraged to establish "joint mechanisms or commissions, as deemed necessary by them, to facilitate cooperation" (article 8(2), article 24). The International Law Commission Draft Articles on the Law of Transboundary Aquifers uses slightly stronger wording by stipulating that, in order to establish and implement plans for the proper management of transboundary aquifers or aquifer systems, "a joint management mechanism shall be established, wherever appropriate". The Water Convention goes even further by requiring that riparian Parties establish joint bodies, and also by setting out the key tasks that those joint bodies must undertake (article 9). SDG indicator 6.5.2 therefore reflects the central importance placed on institutions in international law by including the existence of a "joint body, mechanism or commission" as a key criterion for determining whether or not an agreement or arrangement is operational.

While institutions are seen as critical to supporting the implementation of any arrangement, the SDG indicator 6.5.2 reports demonstrate that there is considerable diversity in the types of institutions that countries have established to suit specific contexts (see Figure 23).[92] As Figure 23 shows, the most common institutional models are the basin or bilateral commissions, which often consist of a high-level decision-making body, such as a council of ministers, a joint committee of governmental representatives, and/or a secretariat. In some instances, countries may be members of both a basin and bilateral commission. Hungary, for example, has established bilateral commissions with Austria, Croatia, Romania, Slovakia, Slovenia, Serbia and Ukraine; while also being a member of the International Commission for the Protection of the Danube River.

The SDG indicator 6.5.2 national reports show that a common feature of joint bodies is the establishment of subsidiary working groups and task teams. These subsidiary bodies have proven to be a particularly important means by which to address new challenges and opportunities. Topics covered by these bodies include flooding, water protection, hydrogeology and groundwater, hydrology, water quality, navigation, institutional development, socioeconomic uses, land management, environment and biodiversity, communication, finance, pollution prevention, accidental pollution, monitoring, data management, legal issues, river regulation, water supply and irrigation, and planning. While showing the wide range of tasks conducted by joint bodies, Figure 24 suggests that data and information exchange, exchange of experiences, and consultations on planned measures are the most common tasks and activities conducted by joint bodies.

SDG indicator 6.5.2 reports also suggest that in some transboundary basins, less detailed institutional arrangements are sufficient to foster transboundary water cooperation (see Box 9).

Figure 23: SDG 6.5.2 national reports – responses to the question: if a joint body exists, which type is in place?

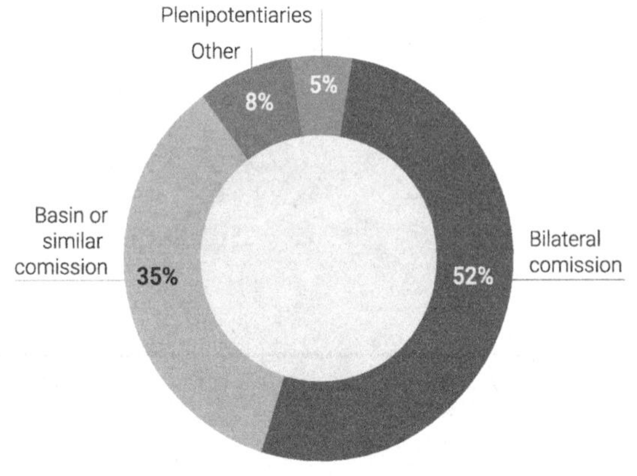

[90] International Law Association. 1976. 'Administration of International Water Resources', Report of the 57th Conference, Madrid, in Slavko Bogdanović, *International Law of Water Resources* (Kluwer 2001), pp. 245-268.

[91] See UNECE. 2018. *Principles for Effective Joint Bodies for Transboundary Water Cooperation.*

[92] See Susanne Schmeier. 2013. *Governing International Watercourses: River Basin Organizations and the Sustainable Government of Internationally Shared Rivers and Lakes.* Routledge. See also UNECE, Capacity for Water Cooperation in Eastern Europe, Caucasus and Central Asia: River Basin Commissions and other Institutions for Transboundary Water Cooperation, UN Doc. ECE/MP.WAT/31, 2009, https://unece.org/fileadmin/DAM/env/water/documents/CWC%20publication%20joint%20bodies.pdf (accessed 2 July 2018).

BOX 8

Defining joint bodies for transboundary water cooperation

According to the UNECE Guide to Implementing the Water Convention (UNECE, 2015): joint commissions are the most common form of joint bodies between riparian countries. The term "joint commission" is a collective term intended to cover also, for example, "joint water authority", "committee", "joint working group", etc. Although the organizational structure of a joint commission may vary according to the specific needs of the riparian countries involved, the majority of them share common features. According to the UNECE Guide to Implementing the Water Convention (2015):

(a) A commission is usually a permanent body meeting at reasonably regular intervals;

(b) A commission is usually composed of representatives of the riparian States, headed usually by officials, authorized for that purpose by governments;

(c) Country representation in a joint commission is not necessarily limited to representatives of water authorities and may also include officials from various ministries and agencies, regional and local or municipal authorities; [*]

(d) A commission may have a decision-making body/ies, an executive body/ies and subsidiary bodies, e.g. working or expert groups, monitoring, data collection and processing units; and

(e) A commission often avails itself of a secretariat. The work of the joint commissions may be supplemented by the establishment of an auditing commission, a network of national offices, a consultative group of donors, an information centre, a training centre or observers. Recent practice shows that joint commissions are increasingly allowing for the participation of representatives from the private sector and the public, including NGOs.

Another form of arrangements for cooperation between riparian States is the institution of "Plenipotentiaries for transboundary waters" [...] A Plenipotentiary for transboundary waters is an official coming from a water management, environmental protection or other relevant national authority, appointed by a national government to facilitate and coordinate the implementation of a transboundary water agreement on behalf of a riparian State. Plenipotentiaries for transboundary waters hold meetings on a regular basis. They may have secretaries to support their work. Plenipotentiaries for transboundary waters are free to establish working groups, call upon expert advice and involve academia, private sector and the public in their activities. Plenipotentiaries for transboundary waters often rely on their work primarily on the ministry/agency they represent, acting as a focal point at the interministerial or interdepartmental level."

UNECE, Guide to Implementing the Water Convention (2015), http://unece.org/index.php?id=33657

* In a context where gender equality is a common principle, gender balance should be promoted when nominating representatives.

BOX 9

The Drin Core Group: a light and flexible institutional structure for basin management

In the case of the Drin Basin, a 'Drin Core Group' was established in 2009 as a light and flexible structure that provides a forum for cooperation among the Parties and key stakeholders, including the Prespa Park Management Committee, Lake Ohrid Watershed Committee, Lake Skadar-Shkoder Commission, UNECE, Global Water Partnership-Mediterranean, and the Mediterranean Information Office for Environment, Culture and Sustainable Development. A key feature of the Drin Core Group is its engagement of other actors in addition to countries. In some instances, this participation may be formalized.

For further information, see http://twrm-med.net/southeastern-europe/supported-processes-and-projects/drin-river-basin/the-institutional-structure-for-the-implementation-of-the-mou/the-drin-core-group.

Figure 24: SDG 6.5.2 national reports – responses to the question: what are the tasks and activities of the joint body?

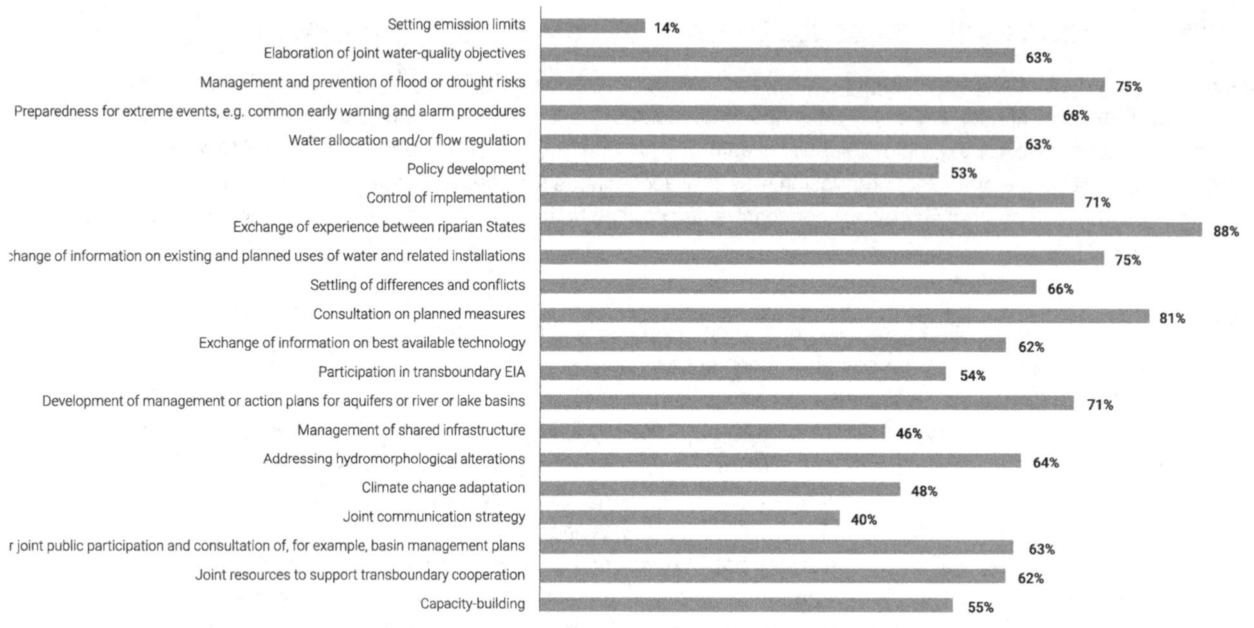

The SDG indicator 6.5.2 national reports have shown that a range of stakeholders may have a role in the activities of joint bodies. In some instances, stakeholders (such as user groups, water utilities and private companies, indigenous groups, community based organizations, research institutions and academia) may be afforded observer status. Figure 25 illustrates the importance that countries place on stakeholder participation, with over three quarters of responses suggesting that stakeholders are involved, to some extent, in transboundary water management. An example of stakeholder engagement in basin management can be seen in the case of the Okavango Delta Management Plan.[93]

To develop the plan, the Permanent Okavango River Basin Water Commission engaged with primary stakeholders, i.e. the riparian communities of the Delta, secondary stakeholders, i.e. other users of the basin, and tertiary stakeholders, i.e. the Governments (Angola, Botswana and Namibia), management institutions, private sector, tourists and international partnerships.

3.3.4. Joint management plan and joint objectives

The presence of a joint or coordinated management plan, or evidence that joint objectives have been set, is a key criterion in measuring operationality under SDG indicator 6.5.2. This requirement closely aligns with the provisions of the Watercourses Convention, the Water Convention and the Draft Articles on the Law of Transboundary Aquifers. For instance, under the Watercourses Convention, countries are, upon a request from another watercourse State, obliged to enter into consultations concerning the management of an international watercourse (article 24(1)). "Management" is defined in the Convention as including "planning the sustainable development of an international watercourse and providing for the implementation of any plans adopted" (article 24(2)(a)). Under the Draft Articles on the Law of Transboundary Aquifers, aquifer countries are, where appropriate,

---

[93] Botswana Department of Environmental Affairs. Okavango Delta Management Plan, http://okacom.org/site-documents/project-reports/odmp-documents/okavango-delta-management-plan/at_download/file (accessed 2 July 2018).

obliged to "establish and implement plans for the proper management of their transboundary aquifers or aquifer systems" (article 14). The need to establish joint water quality objectives and criteria can be found in both the Watercourses Convention (article 21(3)(a)) and the Water Convention (article 3(2)), which also provide planning for emergencies (Watercourses Convention (article 28(4)) and Water Convention (articles 3(1)(j), 14 and 15)).

As reflected in SDG target 6.5, plans are also an important element in implementing IWRM at the national level. However, to date, only an estimated 37 per cent of countries report that basin or aquifer plans based on integrated approaches are being implemented, and 47 per cent of countries report that the preparation or development of such plans has not yet started or has been delayed in the majority of basins or aquifers.[94]

Having such plans in place at the national level, and ensuring their effective harmonization or coordination at the transboundary basin level, can help to implement transboundary basin arrangements. Additionally, progress on transboundary water cooperation might also act as a catalyst for developing and coordinating national plans.

Figure 25: SDG 6.5.2 national reports – responses to the question: are the public or relevant stakeholders involved in transboundary water management in the river or lake basin or aquifer?

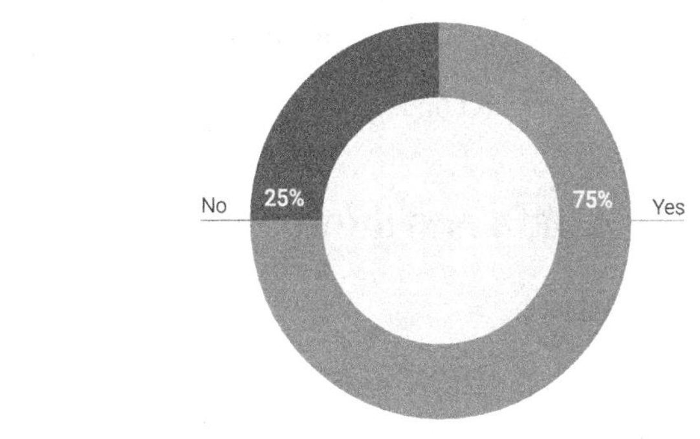

BOX 10

River Basin Management Plans and the EU Water Framework Directive

SDG indicator 6.5.2 reports indicate that there is a concerted effort to develop River Basin Management Plans across Europe, which is due primarily to Directive 2000/60/EC of the European Parliament and of the Council establishing a framework for Community action in the field of water policy (EU Water Framework Directive). The EU Water Framework Directive required Member countries to have in place River Basin Management Plans for all their river basins by 2009 (article 13) and to have updated those plans by 2015. Pursuant to the EU Water Framework Directive, Member countries are encouraged to produce a single River Basin Management Plan for transboundary river basins. Pursuant to this request, international River Basin Management Plans are in place for several transboundary river basins within the EU, including for the Danube, Rhine, Elbe, Ems, Finnish-Norwegian Transboundary Waters, Meuse, Scheldt, Odra and Sava. These plans set out the main pressures impacting these waters, and the measures required in order for the basins to reach or maintain "good ecological status" – as required by the EU Water Framework Directive. Plans must be reviewed and updated every six years.

For further information, see: http://ec.europa.eu/environment/water/participation/map_mc/map.htm.

---

[94] SDG indicator 6.5.1 report (n 5).

Lake Titicaca lies between Andean ranges in a vast basin between Bolivia and Peru. Photo: Winston Mcleod/Creative Commons

3.3.5. Data and information exchange

The exchange of data and information on transboundary waters is key to cooperation, joint decisions and joint management. The Water Convention (articles 6 and 13), the Watercourses Convention (article 9) and the Draft Articles on the Law of Transboundary Aquifers (article 8) include a firm obligation on countries to exchange such data and information on the conditions of a particular transboundary river, lake or aquifer system. In addition, under all three instruments, countries are obligated to apply their best efforts to respond to requests for data and information that are not readily available.

Therefore, SDG indicator 6.5.2 operationality criteria include whether basin countries exchange data and information at least once per year. As illustrated in Figure 26, the SDG indicator 6.5.2 reports show that countries exchange data and information on a wide range of topics.

Countries understand the benefits of data and information exchange, which they listed in the SDG indicator 6.5.2 reports as: providing an understanding of the main pressures relating to a particular transboundary water system; allowing for better appreciation of the issues and problems faced by other basin countries; highlighting improved possibilities for early warning and alarm systems; developing a better understanding of data gaps; helping harmonize methodologies and standards for data gathering, leading to better project design; and offering more effective river basin management planning.

BOX 11

Developing a Binational Master Plan for the Titicaca-Desaguadero-Poopó-Salar De Coipasa Basin (Bolivia and Peru)

Supported by the Global Environment Facility, Bolivia and Peru are in the process of updating their Binational Master Plan for the Titicaca-Desaguadero-Poopó-Salar De Coipasa (TDPS). In 1992, the two countries established the Binational Autonomous Authority for the Water System of Lake Titicaca, Desaguadero River, Lake Poopó and Salar de Coipasa (ALT), which was charged with implementing the first Binational Master Plan adopted in 1991. While significant progress has been made towards the sustainable management of the basin, Bolivia and Peru are updating the plan in order to develop a comprehensive analysis of the transboundary situation in the TDPS, including its vulnerability to extreme events, as well as an agreed vision, mission, objectives and main lines of action for the TDPS.

For further information, see: www.alt-perubolivia.org.

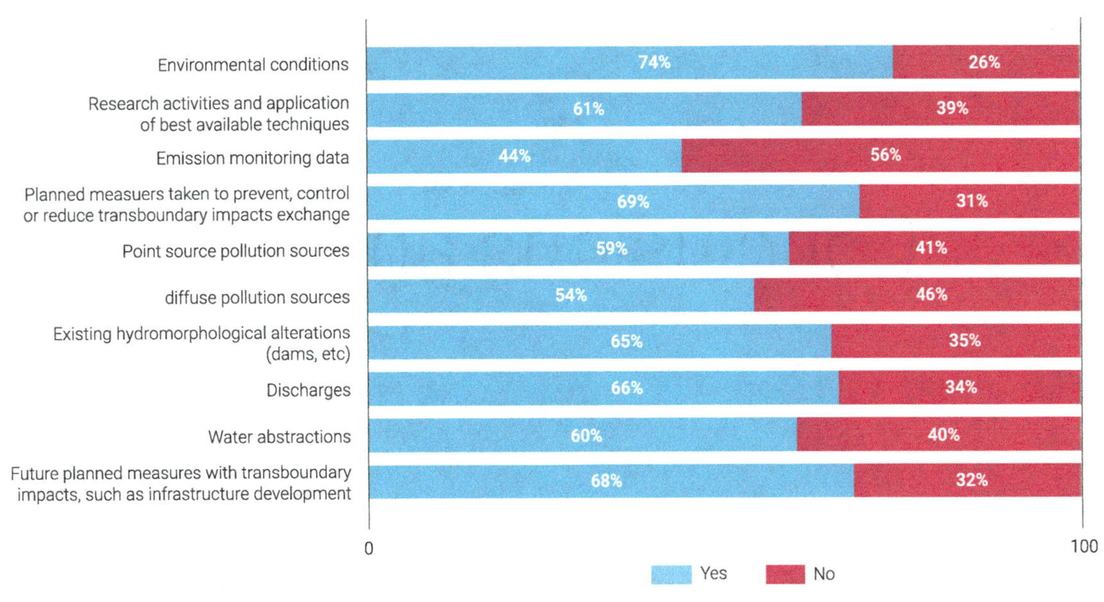

BOX 12

Fostering cooperation over the North-West Sahara Aquifer System through data and information exchange

The North-West Sahara Aquifer System (NWSAS) shared between Algeria, Libya and Tunisia is one of the major North African transboundary aquifer systems. Exploitation of this multi-layered non-renewable system has caused a steep decline in the aquifer's artesian pressure, groundwater salinization, and loss of natural oases. In 2002, the three countries reached an agreement to establish a Consultation Mechanism, with a particular focus on data collection and exchange related to the aquifer system, as well as the dissemination of those data and information to decision makers. This cooperation has led to improved knowledge of the NWSAS. Effective data gathering and exchange has allowed the countries to develop sophisticated modelling tools for improved multi-stakeholder decision-making.

Conclusions and next steps

An aerial view of the Niger river near Ansongo, in eastern Mali. UN Photo/Marco Dormino

4.1. Contribution of SDG indicator 6.5.2 to transboundary water cooperation

The introduction of SDG indicator 6.5.2 into the SDG framework marks an important step forward in monitoring and progressing transboundary water cooperation. For the first time, a country-based process provides the basis upon which to assess the coverage of operational arrangements across the world's transboundary basins. As these transboundary basins are home to over 40 per cent of the world's population, such an assessment significantly contributes to monitoring IWRM implementation, and the goal of achieving clean water and sanitation for all by 2030. As the only target to directly focus on transboundary water cooperation, SDG target 6.5 – and SDG indicator 6.5.2 in particular – also provide an important complement to the many other SDGs that rely, at least in part, on transboundary cooperation.

At the national level, the SDG indicator 6.5.2 monitoring process provides impetus for countries to assess the current status of cooperation with neighbouring countries and identify any knowledge gaps regarding their transboundary cooperation. Such an assessment can offer a basis upon which countries might set national targets towards ensuring that transboundary basins are covered by operational arrangements. By coordinating and harmonizing reporting on SDG indicators 6.5.1 and 6.5.2, the reporting process can also provide a fuller picture of IWRM implementation at all levels.

At the basin level, where countries sharing a particular river, lake or aquifer collaborate to report on SDG indicator 6.5.2, the monitoring process offers a transparent and uniform means by which to measure progress and set targets. Joint bodies and regional organizations can play a key role in advancing such a monitoring process in a coordinated manner.

More generally, SDG indicator 6.5.2 monitoring offers the opportunity to locate any gaps and hotspots, and areas where more efforts are needed to either revise existing arrangements to make them operational or adopt new arrangements that embody key principles of IWRM and international law. SDG indicator 6.5.2 also provides an opportunity to look at how advanced transboundary water cooperation is in different areas. In so doing, monitoring can point to areas where lessons and experiences could be shared across transboundary basins.

Moving forward, three-yearly monitoring cycles of SDG indicator 6.5.2 will allow countries to measure progress towards transboundary water cooperation and, together with 6.5.1, the target of implementing IWRM at all levels by 2030. One important feature of the methodology in this regard is the indicator template. By asking countries to report not just the indicator value but on all their transboundary basins – even those where operational arrangements are not in place – and to provide detailed data on the status of each indicator criteria within all their transboundary basins, this template enables progress towards operationality to be measured over time. Additionally, the integrated approach to monitoring SDG 6, and fostering linkages to other water-related SDGs, offers the opportunity to better understand what progress made in transboundary water cooperation means for other SDGs.

Communication between countries and custodian agencies and capacity-building will be essential to improving national data. For example, capacity-building initiatives that utilize global data sources, such as ISARM and TWAP, to more accurately identify and delineate transboundary basins can assist greatly in enhancing national reports. As the initial reporting exercise has illustrated, these efforts are especially needed for transboundary aquifers, where data at the national level are either lacking or not widely accessible. Promoting data exchange and harmonization across countries sharing the same transboundary rivers, lakes or aquifers would provide an additional opportunity to strengthen reporting on SDG indicator 6.5.2. However, as observed during the first reporting cycle, riparian countries do not always reach a consensus. Nevertheless, reporting can provide a basis for fostering discussions on transboundary water cooperation within the wider SDG framework.

4.2. What does the first SDG indicator 6.5.2 reporting exercise tell us?

At the global level, the results of the first SDG indicator 6.5.2 reporting exercise suggest that more effort is needed to increase the coverage of operational arrangements across the world's transboundary basins. While notable progress has been made in several regions, the global picture suggests that many transboundary basins are not covered by an operational arrangement. The situation is particularly stark for transboundary aquifers, where only a few aquifer-specific arrangements are in place, or aquifers are only partially covered by river or lake basin arrangements.

The regional analysis of operational arrangements for transboundary water cooperation suggests that, while cooperation is evident in all regions, there is significant regional variation in terms of transboundary basin areas covered by operational arrangements. Europe and Northern America, and sub-Saharan Africa, show the highest coverage levels of operational arrangements, particularly in relation to transboundary river and lakes. Although progress in other regions is less advanced, there are many instances where countries are making concerted efforts to advance their transboundary water cooperation.

4.3. Accelerating progress on transboundary water cooperation

Giordano *et al.* suggest that the number of arrangements for transboundary basins has increased over recent decades at an average rate of three per year. Following a similar trajectory, and assuming that these arrangements are operational, this would suggest that an additional 36 transboundary arrangements might be adopted by 2030. Even if these arrangements covered entire basins, this would still leave a significant gap in the coverage of the world's transboundary basins.

A particularly critical challenge, but also an opportunity, is to ensure that transboundary aquifers are appropriately covered by operational arrangements. Despite the numerous services that groundwater provides for both humans and ecosystems, operational arrangements for transboundary aquifers are still rare around the world. Transboundary aquifers entered late on the scientific and political agendas, probably to a large extent on account of the hidden nature and the political unattractiveness of groundwater. This "invisible" resource therefore often lacks the attention that it deserves.

It is therefore clear that progress in transboundary water cooperation must be dramatically accelerated to ensure that target 6.5 is reached by 2030. Several concerted actions can be taken:

- **Capitalize on the experience and outputs of the first SDG indicator 6.5.2 reporting exercise.** This exercise has demonstrated that SDG indicator 6.5.2 operationality criteria and its associated reporting template offer a robust methodology for monitoring transboundary water cooperation across a diverse range of settings. Such diversity is reflected in the many different cooperative contexts captured by the criteria. By drawing upon the success of the first reporting exercise, while recognizing the limitations and gaps, SDG indicator 6.5.2 monitoring can play an important role in advancing transboundary cooperation. To this end, it is important that countries and regions where reporting levels are currently low engage in reporting exercises. Moreover, SDG indicator 6.5.2 reports should be used to set national and basin-specific targets related to transboundary water cooperation. Finally, cooperation can be supported by drawing upon SDG indicator 6.5.2 to share knowledge and experiences of both achievements and challenges at the regional and global levels.

- **Invest in projects to support joint acquisition/ exchange of data and enhance information and knowledge on transboundary basins.** Such projects not only produce an advanced level of local knowledge (and thus help define issues and priorities), they also constitute the simplest initial step in transboundary cooperation and can thus pave the way for next steps that may be more politically sensitive.[95] Such projects are particularly important for transboundary aquifers, where there is a clear need to deepen knowledge and understanding.

- **Build upon the Watercourses Convention, the Water Convention and the Draft Articles on the Law of Transboundary Aquifers.** Where operational arrangements are lacking, these instruments offer an important basis upon which new arrangements can be negotiated or existing arrangements can be revised. The entry into force of the Watercourses Convention and the opening of the Water Convention to all countries are significant milestones in advancing transboundary water cooperation. The institutional framework of the Water Convention also offers an important platform for countries to share experiences in transboundary water cooperation, and reach a common understanding on how to advance such cooperation based on fundamental principles of international law and existing good practices.

- **Couple efforts to enhance transboundary water cooperation with other critical issues related to sustainability, climate change, poverty alleviation, and peace and security.** Transboundary water cooperation offers multiple benefits that go beyond water. Coupling efforts and fostering synergies between these linked issues offers an important means by which to most effectively advance transboundary water cooperation.

- **Increase financing for transboundary water cooperation, including enabling the use of climate finance for transboundary initiatives.** The negotiation, adoption and implementation of operational arrangements can be both costly and resource-intensive. However, 23 out of 100 countries suggest that for their main transboundary basins, no specific funding is allocated at the national level and no other regular resources are in place to finance transboundary cooperation.[96] Similarly, there is a recognized need to increase overall investment in water and sanitation to achieve SDG 6.[97] More national and international funds should be mobilized to support transboundary cooperation, especially since transboundary water cooperation can offer significant economic benefits, thus providing an important incentive for investing in operational arrangements. Given that climate change impacts have a direct effect on water, finance available for the mitigation of and adaptation to climate change offer an important avenue to fund transboundary water management. However, most of the available international climate financing sources do not currently foresee mechanisms to finance transboundary initiatives.

---

[95] For instance, this approach underpins the Transboundary Diagnostic Analysis promoted as the first step for projects funded under the International Waters component of the Global Environment Facility (GEF).

[96] SDG indicator 6.5.1 report.

[97] SDG 6 Synthesis Report 2018 on Water and Sanitation.

Annex I Table of countries with breakdown of SDG 6.5.2 indicator value, river and lake basin value, and aquifer value for each

Country name	Rivers & lakes component (%)	Aquifers component (%)	SDG indicator 6.5.2 (%)
Afghanistan	51.7	-	-
Albania	66.8	89.3	75.6
Algeria	0	-	-
Andorra	4.4	-	-
Angola	100	15.2	78.9
Armenia	0.1	0	0.1
Austria	100	100	100
Belgium	100	100	100
Benin	96.3	49.2	81.5
Bosnia and Herzegovina	96.1	73.3	92.6
Botswana	100	100	100
Brazil	98.2	0	62.4
Bulgaria	100	97.6	99.6
Burkina Faso	93.6	-	-
Burundi	92.0	79.4	88.3
Canada	100	0	87.9
Chad	48.3	53.1	50.4
Chile	0	0	0
Colombia	1.1	-	-
Côte d'Ivoire	18.0	-	-
Croatia	100	-	-
Czech Republic	100	100	100
Democratic Republic of the Congo	99.6	-	-
Dominican Republic	0	0	0
Ecuador	100	100	100
El Salvador	0	0	0
Equatorial Guinea	0	N	0
Estonia	100	100	100
Finland	100	N	100
France	53.1	-	-
Gabon	0	0	0
Gambia	99.0	0	49.0
Georgia	0	0	0
Germany	100	100	100

Country name	Rivers & lakes component (%)	Aquifers component (%)	SDG indicator 6.5.2 (%)
Ghana	88.4	95.7	91.1
Greece	58.1	-	-
Guinea	66.8	-	-
Honduras	0	0	0
Hungary	100	100	100
Iraq	17.3	0	13.5
Ireland	100	100	100
Italy	100	100	100
Jordan	61.7	13.9	21.9
Kazakhstan	100	0	72.4
Kenya	35.9	0	26.8
Kuwait	N	-	-
Latvia	100	95.0	97.3
Lesotho	100	0	50.0
Lithuania	26.8	50.2	35.0
Luxembourg	100	100	100
Malaysia	13.4	-	-
Mali	99.9	60.7	75.3
Mexico	2.3	0	1.3
Monaco	N	-	-
Montenegro	84.2	0	79.5
Morocco	0	0	0
Namibia	100	100	100
Netherlands	100	100	100
Niger	100	75.0	89.6
Nigeria	100	-	-
Norway	59.5	54.4	59.5
Paraguay	100	0	50.9
Peru	14.1	-	-
Poland	72.3	100	-
Portugal	100	-	-
Qatar	N	0	0
Republic of Korea	0	0	0
Romania	100	100	100

Country name	Rivers & lakes component (%)	Aquifers component (%)	SDG indicator 6.5.2 (%)
Senegal	100	0	34.1
Serbia	92.3	78.1	90.0
Sierra Leone	7.0	N	7.0
Slovakia	100	100	100
Slovenia	100	100	100
Somalia	0	0	0
South Africa	100	-	-
Spain	100	-	-
Sweden	-	100	-
Switzerland	93.5	-	-
The former Yugoslav Republic of Macedonia	13.6	-	-
Togo	55.6	76.0	60.2
Tunisia	0	100	80.5
Uganda	97.5	0	83.6
Ukraine	36.9	-	-
United Kingdom of Great Britain and Northern Ireland	0	0	0
Uzbekistan	59.3	-	-
Venezuela (Bolivarian Republic of)	7.0	0	3.5
Zambia	76.8	0	70.0
Zimbabwe	76.2	-	-

Note:

N: *Non-relevant: indicates that the figure is not available because the indicator – as defined for the global monitoring – does not apply to the circumstances of the specific country, and therefore is not reported.*

Dashes: *indicate that the figure is not available because the country response needs clarification.*

Annex II Template for reporting

Section I. Calculation of SDG indicator 6.5.2

a.   Methodology

This section describes how to calculate the Sustainable Development Goal global indicator 6.5.2, which is defined as "the proportion of transboundary basin area with an operational arrangement for water cooperation". The information gathered in section II will help with completing this section. The step-by-step monitoring methodology for SDG indicator 6.5.2, developed by UNECE and UNESCO in the framework of UN-Water, can be referred to for details on the necessary data, the definitions and the calculation.

The value of the indicator at the national level is derived by **adding up the surface area in a country of those transboundary surface water catchments and transboundary aquifers (i.e. "transboundary basins") that are covered by an operational arrangement and dividing the obtained area by the aggregate total area in a country of all transboundary basins (both catchments and aquifers).**

Transboundary basins are basins of transboundary waters, that is, of any surface waters (notably rivers and lakes) or groundwaters which mark, cross or are located on boundaries between by two or more States. For the purpose of calculating this indicator, for a transboundary river or lake, the basin area is determined by the extent of its catchment. For groundwater, the area to be considered is the extent of the aquifer.

An **"arrangement for water cooperation"** is a bilateral or multilateral treaty, convention, agreement or other formal arrangement among riparian countries that provides a framework for cooperation on transboundary water management.

For an arrangement to be considered **"operational"**, all the following criteria need to be fulfilled:

— There is a joint body, joint mechanism or commission (e.g. a river basin organization) for transboundary cooperation
— There are regular (at least once per year) formal communications between riparian countries in the form of meetings (either at the political or technical level)
— There is a joint or coordinated water management plan(s), or joint objectives have been set, and
— There is a regular (at least once per year) exchange of data and information.

b.   Calculation of indicator 6.5.2

Please list in the tables below the transboundary basins (rivers and lakes and aquifers) in your country's territory and provide the following information for each of them:

— the country/ies with which the basin is shared
— the surface area of these basins (the catchment of rivers or lakes and the aquifer in the case of groundwater) within the territory of your country (in km^2)
— the surface area of these basins within the territory of your country which is covered by a cooperation arrangement that is operational according to the above criteria (please consider the replies to the questions in section II, in particular questions 1, 2, 3, 4 and 6).

If an operational arrangement is in place only for a sub-basin or a portion of a basin, please list this sub-basin just after the transboundary basin it is part of. If there is an operational arrangement for the whole basin, do not list sub-basins in the table below.

---

[98] Available at http://unwater.org/publications/step-step-methodology-monitoring-transboundary-cooperation-6-5-2/

Transboundary basin (river or lake) [please add rows as needed]

Name of the transboundary basin/sub-basin	Countries shared with	Surface area of the basin/sub-basin (in km²) within the territory of the country	Name of the transboundary basin/sub-basin (in km²) covered by an operational arrangement within the territory of the country
Total surface area of transboundary basins/sub-basins of rivers and lakes covered by operational arrangements within the territory of the country (in km²) [A] (do not double count sub-basins)			
Total surface area of transboundary basins of rivers and lakes within the territory of the country (in km²) [B] (do not double count sub-basins)			

Transboundary aquifers [please add rows as needed]

Name of the transboundary aquifer	Countries shared with	Surface area of the basin/sub-basin (in km²)[99] within the territory of the country	Name of the transboundary basin/sub-basin (in km²) covered by an operational arrangement within the territory of the country
Total surface area of transboundary aquifers covered by operational arrangements within the territory of the country (in km²) [C]			
Total surface area of transboundary aquifers within the territory of the country (in km²) [D]			

Indicator value for the country

$((A + C) / (B + D)) \times 100\% =$

Additional information

If the respondent has comments that clarify assumptions or interpretations made for the calculation, or the level of certainty of the spatial information, please write them here:

Spatial information

If a map (or maps) of the transboundary surface water catchments and transboundary aquifers (i.e. "transboundary basins") is available, please attach them. Ideally, shapefiles of the basin and aquifer delineations that can be viewed in Geographical Information Systems should be sent.

---

[93] For a transboundary aquifer, the extent is derived from the aquifer system delineation, which commonly relies on information of the subsurface (notably the extent of geological formations). As a general rule, the delineation of aquifer systems is based on the delineation of the extent of the hydraulically connected water-bearing geological formations. Aquifer systems are three-dimensional objects and the aquifer area taken into account is the projection on the land surface of the system. Ideally, when different aquifer systems not hydraulically connected are vertically superposed, the different relevant projected areas are to be considered separately, unless the different aquifer systems are managed conjunctively.

Section II. Information on each transboundary basin or group of basins

Please complete this second section for each transboundary basin (river, lake or aquifer) or for group of basins covered by the same agreement or arrangement and where conditions are similar. It might also be convenient to group basins or sub-basins for which your country's share is very small.[100] In some instances, you may provide information on both a basin and one or more of its sub-basins, for example, where you have agreements[101] on both the basin and its sub-basin. You may coordinate your responses with other States with which your country shares the basin or aquifer or even prepare a joint report for shared basins. General information on transboundary water management at the national level should be provided in section III and not repeated here.

Please reproduce the whole of section II with its questions for each transboundary basin, river, lake or aquifer, or group of basins for which you will provide a reply.

Name of the transboundary basin, river, lake or aquifer, or group thereof, list of the riparian States, and country's share of the basin: [fill in]

1. Is there one or more transboundary (bilateral or multilateral) agreement(s) or arrangement(s) on this basin?

> One or more agreements or arrangements exist and are in force
> Agreement or arrangement developed but not in force
> Agreement or arrangement developed, but not in force for all riparians

Please insert the name of the agreement or agreements or arrangements: [fill in]

> Agreement or arrangement is under development
> No agreement
> *If there is no agreement or arrangement or it is not in force, please explain briefly why not and provide information on any plans to address the situation:* [fill in]

If there is no agreement or arrangement and no joint body for the transboundary basin, river, lake or aquifer then jump to question 4; if there is no agreement, but a joint body then go to question 3.

Questions 2 and 3 to be completed for each bilateral or multilateral agreement or arrangement in force in the transboundary basin (river, lake or aquifer) or group of basins or sub-basins.

2. (a) Does this agreement or arrangement specify the basin area subject to cooperation?

> Yes
> No

If yes, does it cover the entire basin, or group of basins, and all riparian States?

> Yes
> No

If not, what does it cover? [fill in]

---

[100] In principle, section II should be submitted for every transboundary basin, river, lake or aquifer, in the country, but States may decide to group basins in which their share is small or leave out basins in which their share is very minor, e.g., below 1 per cent.
[101] In section II, "agreement" covers all kinds of treaties, conventions and agreements ensuring cooperation in the field of transboundary waters. Section II can also be completed for other types of arrangements, such as memorandums of understanding.

Or, if the agreement or arrangement relates to a sub-basin, does it cover the entire sub-basin?

Yes
No

Which States (including your own) are bound by the agreement or arrangement? *(Please list):* [fill in]

(b) Are aquifers (or groundwater bodies) covered by the agreement/arrangement?

Yes
No

(c) What is the sectoral scope of the agreement or arrangement?

All water uses
A single water use or sector
Several water uses or sectors

If one or several water uses or sectors, please list (check as appropriate):

Water uses or sectors
Industry
Agriculture
Transport (e.g., navigation)
Households
Energy: hydropower and other energy types
Tourism
Nature protection
Other *(please list):* [fill in]

(d) What topics or subjects of cooperation are included in the agreement or arrangement?

Procedural and institutional issues
Dispute and conflict prevention and resolution
Institutional cooperation (joint bodies)
Consultation on planned measures
Mutual assistance

Topics of cooperation
Joint vision and management objectives
Joint significant water management issues
Navigation
Environmental protection (ecosystem)
Water quality
Water quantity or allocation
Cooperation in addressing floods
Cooperation in addressing droughts
Climate change adaptation

Monitoring and exchange
Joint assessments
Data collection and exchange
Joint monitoring
Maintenance of joint pollution inventories
Elaboration of joint water quality objectives
Common early warning and alarm procedures

Exchange of experience between riparian States
Exchange of information on planned measures

Joint planning and management
Development of joint regulations on specific topics
Development of international or joint river, lake or aquifer basin management or action plans
Management of shared infrastructure
Development of shared infrastructure
Other *(please list)*: [fill in]

(e)   What are the main difficulties and challenges that your country faces with the agreement or arrangement and its implementation, if any *(please describe, if applicable)*: [fill in]

(f)   What are the main achievements in implementing the agreement or arrangement and what were the keys to achieving such success? [fill in]

(g)   Please attach a copy of the agreement or arrangement or provide the web address of the document *(please attach document or insert web address, if applicable)*: [fill in]

3. Is your country a member of an operational joint body or joint bodies for this agreement/arrangement?

Yes
No
If no, why not? (please explain): [fill in]

Where there is a joint body (or bodies)

(a)   If there is a joint body, which kind of joint body *(please tick one)*?

Plenipotentiaries
Bilateral commission
Basin or similar commission
Other *(please describe)*: [fill in]

(b)   Does the joint body cover the entire transboundary basin or sub-basin, river, lake or aquifer, or group of basins, and all riparian States?

Yes
No

(c)   Which States (including your own) are a member of the joint body? *(Please list)* [fill in]

(d)   Does the joint body have any of the following features *(please tick the ones applicable)*?

A secretariat
If the secretariat is a permanent one, is it a joint secretariat or does each country host its own secretariat? (Please describe): [fill in]
A subsidiary body or bodies
Please list (e.g., working groups on specific topics): [fill in]
Other features *(please list)*: [fill in]

(e)   What are the tasks and activities of this joint body?[102]

Identification of pollution sources
Data collection and exchange
Joint monitoring
Maintenance of joint pollution inventories
Setting emission limits
Elaboration of joint water quality objectives
Management and prevention of flood or drought risks
Preparedness for extreme events, e.g., common early warning and alarm procedures
Water allocation and/or flow regulation
Policy development
Control of implementation
Exchange of experience between riparian States
Exchange of information on existing and planned
uses of water and related installations
Settling of differences and conflicts
Consultations on planned measures
Exchange of information on best available technology
Participation in transboundary environmental impact assessment (EIA)
Development of river, lake or aquifer basin management or action plans
Management of shared infrastructure
Addressing hydromorphological alterations
Climate change adaptation
Joint communication strategy
Basin-wide or joint public participation and consultation of, for example, basin management plans
Joint resources to support transboundary cooperation
Capacity-building
Any other tasks *(please list)*: [fill in]

(f)   What are the main difficulties and challenges that your country faces with the operation of the joint body, if any?

Governance issues
Please describe, if any: [fill in]

Unexpected planning delays
Please describe, if any: [fill in]

Lack of resources
Please describe, if true: [fill in]

Lack of mechanism for implementing measures
Please describe, if true: [fill in]

Lack of effective measures
Please describe, if true: [fill in]

Unexpected extreme events
Please describe, if any: [fill in]

Lack of information and reliable forecasts
Please describe, if any: [fill in]
Others *(please list and describe, as appropriate)*: [fill in]

---

[102] This may include tasks according to the agreement or tasks added by the joint body, or its subsidiaries. Both tasks which joint bodies coordinate and tasks which they implement should be included.

(g) If not all riparian States are members of the joint body, how does the body cooperate with them?

No cooperation
They have observer status
Other *(please describe)*: [fill in]

(h) Does the joint body or its subsidiary bodies meet regularly?
Yes
No
If yes, how frequently does it meet? [fill in]

(i) What are the main achievements with regards to the joint body? [fill in]

(j) Are representatives of international organizations invited to the meetings of the joint body (or bodies) as observers?

Yes
No

(k) Did the joint body ever invite a coastal State to cooperate?

Yes
No
If yes, please give details. If no, why not? [fill in]

4. Is there a joint or coordinated management plan (such as an action plan or a common strategy) or have joint objectives been set specifically on the transboundary waters subject to cooperation?

Yes
No
If yes, please provide further details: [fill in]

5. How is the transboundary basin, river, lake or aquifer protected, including the protection of ecosystems, in the context of sustainable and rational water use?

Afforestation
Restoration of ecosystems
Environmental flow norms
Groundwater measures (e.g., protection zones)
Other measures *(please list)*: [fill in]

6. (a) Does your country exchange information and data with other riparian States in the basin?

Yes
No

(b) If yes, on what subjects are information and data exchanged?

Environmental conditions
Research activities and application of best available techniques
Emission monitoring data
Planned measures taken to prevent, control or reduce transboundary impacts
Point source pollution sources
Diffuse pollution sources
Existing hydromorphological alterations (e.g., dams)
Discharges

Water abstractions
Future planned measures with transboundary impacts, such as infrastructure development
Other subjects *(please list)*: [fill in]

(c)   Is there a shared database or information platform?

Yes
No

(d)   Is the database publicly available?

Yes
No
If yes, please provide the web address: [fill in]

(e)   What are the main difficulties and challenges to data exchange, if applicable? *(please describe)*: [fill in]

(f)   What are the main benefits of data exchange on the transboundary waters subject to cooperation? *(please describe)*: [fill in]

7. Do the riparian States carry out joint monitoring in the transboundary basin, river, lake or aquifer?

Yes
No

(a)   If yes, what does the joint monitoring cover?

	Covered?	Hydrological	Ecological	Chemical
Border surface waters				
Surface waters in the entire basin				
Surface waters on the main watercourse				
Connected aquifers (or groundwaters)				
Unconnected aquifers (or groundwaters)				

(b)   If joint monitoring is carried out, how is this done?

National monitoring stations connected through a network or common stations
Joint and agreed methodologies
Joint sampling
Common monitoring network
Common agreed parameters

(c)   Please describe the main achievements regarding joint monitoring, if any: [fill in]

(d)   Please describe any difficulties experienced with joint monitoring: [fill in]

8. Do the riparian States carry out joint assessment of the transboundary basin, river, lake or aquifer?

Yes
No
If yes, please provide the date of the last or only assessment, the frequency and scope (e.g., surface waters or groundwaters only, pollution sources, etc.) of the assessment: [fill in]

9. Have the riparian States agreed to use joint water quality standards?

Yes
No
If yes, is the basis an international or regional standard (please specify which) or has it been adapted from the national standards of the riparian States? [fill in]

10. What are the measures implemented to prevent or limit the transboundary impact of accidental pollution?
Notification and communication
Coordinated or joint alarm system for accidental water pollution
Other *(please list):* [fill in]
No measures
If not, why not? What difficulties does your country face in putting in place such measures? [fill in]

11. What are the measures implemented to prevent or limit the transboundary impact of extreme weather events?

Notification and communication
Coordinated or joint alarm system for floods
Coordinated or joint alarm system for droughts
Joint climate change adaptation strategy
Joint disaster risk reduction strategy
Other *(please list):* [fill in]

No measures
If not, why not? What difficulties does your country face in putting in place such measures? [fill in]

12. Are procedures in place for mutual assistance in case of a critical situation?

Yes
No
If yes, please provide a brief summary: [fill in]

13. Are the public or relevant stakeholders involved in transboundary water management in the river or lake basin or aquifer?
Yes
No
If yes, how? (please tick all applicable) (Please note: If your country is a Party to the Convention on Access to Information, Public Participation in Decision-making and Access to Justice in Environmental Matters (Aarhus Convention), you may refer to your country's report under that Convention.):

Stakeholders have observer status in a joint body
If yes, please specify the stakeholders for each joint body: [fill in]

Availability of information to the public
Consultation on planned measures or River Basin Management Plans[103]
Public involvement
Other *(please specify):* [fill in]

> Please remember to complete section II for each of the transboundary basins (rivers, lakes or aquifers).
> Please also remember to attach copies of agreements, if any.

---

[103] Or, where applicable, aquifer management plans.

Section III.   General information on transboundary water management at the national level

In this section, you are requested to provide general information on transboundary water management at the national level. Information on specific transboundary basins (rivers, lakes or aquifers) and agreements should be presented in section II and not repeated here.

---

1. (a)   Does your country's national legislation refer to measures to prevent, control and reduce any transboundary impact?

Yes
No
If yes, list the main national legislation: [fill in]

(b)   Do your country's national policies, action plans and strategies refer to measures to prevent, control and reduce any transboundary impact?

Yes
No
If yes, list the main national policies, action plans and strategies: [fill in]

(c)   Does your country's legislation provide for the following principles?

Precautionary principle	Yes	No
Polluter pays principle	Yes	No
Sustainable development	Yes	No

(d)   Does your country have a national licensing or permitting system for wastewater discharges and other point source pollution *(e.g., in industry, mining, energy, municipal, wastewater management or other sectors)*?

Yes
No
If yes, for which sectors? (please list): [fill in]
If not, please explain why not (giving the most important reasons) or provide information if there are plans to introduce a licensing or permitting system: [fill in]

If your country has a licensing system, does the system provide for setting emission limits based on best available technology?
Yes
No

(e)   Are the authorized discharges monitored and controlled?

Yes
No
If yes, how? (Please tick the ones applicable):
Monitoring of discharges
Monitoring of physical and chemical impacts on water
Monitoring of ecological impacts on water
Conditions on permits
Inspectorate

Other means *(please list):* [fill in]
If your country does not have a discharge monitoring system, please explain why not or provide information if there are plans to introduce a discharge monitoring system: [fill in]

(f) What are the main measures that your country takes to reduce diffuse sources of water pollution on trans-boundary waters *(e.g., from agriculture, transport, forestry or aquaculture)*? The measures listed below relate to agriculture, but other sectors may be more significant. Please be sure to include these under "others":

Legislative measures
Norm for uses of fertilizers
Norms for uses of manure
Bans on or norms for use of pesticides
Others *(please list)*: [fill in]

Economic and financial measures
Monetary incentives
Environmental taxes (such as fertilizer taxes)
Others *(please list)*: [fill in]

Agricultural extension services

Technical measures
Source control measures
Crop rotation
Tillage control
Winter cover crops
Others (please list): [fill in]
Other measures
Buffer/filter strips
Wetland reconstruction
Sedimentation traps
Chemical measures
Others *(please list)*: [fill in]

Other types of measures
If yes, please list: [fill in]

(g) What are the main measures that your country takes to enhance water efficiency? Please tick as appropriate *(not all might be relevant)*

A regulatory system regarding water abstraction
Monitoring and control of abstractions
Water rights are clearly defined
Water allocation priorities are listed
Water-saving technologies
Advanced irrigation techniques
Demand management activities
Other means *(please list)*

(h) Does your country apply the ecosystems?

Yes
No
If yes, please describe how: [fill in]

(i) Does your country take specific measures to prevent the pollution of groundwaters?

Yes
No
If yes, please list the most important measures: [fill in]

2. Does your country require transboundary environmental impact assessment (EIA)?

Yes
No

Does your country have procedures for transboundary EIA?
Yes
No
If yes, please make reference to the legislative basis (please insert the name and section of the relevant laws):
[fill in]

3. Does your country have transboundary agreements or arrangements for the protection and/or management of transboundary waters (i.e., surface waters or aquifers), whether bilateral, multilateral and/or at the basin level?

Yes
No
If yes, list the bilateral, multilateral and basin agreements (listing for each of the countries concerned): [fill in]

Section IV.   Final questions

1. **What are the main challenges your country faces in cooperating on transboundary waters?** (*Please describe*): [fill in]

2. **What have been the main achievements in cooperating on transboundary waters? What were the keys to achieving that success?** (*Please describe concrete examples*): [fill in]

3. **Please include any additional information on the process of preparing the report (e.g., whether there was an exchange or consultation within the joint body or with riparian countries), in particular which institutions have been consulted** (*please describe*): [fill in]

4. **If you have any other comments, please add them here** (*insert comments*): [fill in]

5. **Name and contact details of the person(s) who filled out the questionnaire** (*please insert*): [fill in]

Date: [fill in]   Signature: [fill in]

Thank you very much for taking the time to complete this report.

List of boxes and figures

LEARN MORE ABOUT PROGRESS TOWARDS SDG 6

6 CLEAN WATER AND SANITATION

SDG 6 expands the MDG focus on drinking water and basic sanitation to include the more holistic management of water, wastewater and ecosystem resources, acknowledging the importance of an enabling environment. Bringing these aspects together is an initial step towards addressing sector fragmentation and enabling coherent and sustainable management. It is also a major step towards a sustainable water future.

The monitoring of progress towards SDG 6 is a means to making this happen. High-quality data help policy- and decision makers at all levels of government to identify challenges and opportunities, to set priorities for more effective and efficient implementation, to communicate progress and ensure accountability, and to generate political, public and private sector support for further investment.

In 2016–2018, following the adoption of the global indicator framework, the UN-Water Integrated Monitoring Initiative focused on establishing the global baseline for all SDG 6 global indicators, which is essential for effective follow-up and review of progress towards SDG 6. Below is an overview of the resultant indicator reports produced in 2017–2018. UN-Water has also produced the SDG 6 Synthesis Report 2018 on Water and Sanitation, which, building on baseline data, addresses the cross-cutting nature of water and sanitation and the many interlinkages within SDG 6 and across the 2030 Agenda, and discusses ways to accelerate progress towards SDG 6.

Progress on Drinking Water, Sanitation and Hygiene – 2017 Update and SDG Baselines (including data on SDG indicators 6.1.1 and 6.2.1) By WHO and UNICEF	One of the most important uses of water is for drinking and hygiene purposes. A safely managed sanitation chain is essential to protecting the health of individuals and communities and the environment. By monitoring use of drinking water and sanitation services, policy- and decision makers can find out who has access to safe water and a toilet with handwashing facilities at home, and who requires it. Learn more about the baseline situation for SDG indicators 6.1.1 and 6.2.1 here: http://www.unwater.org/publication_categories/whounicef-joint-monitoring-programme-for-water-supply-sanitation-hygiene-jmp/.
Progress on Safe Treatment and Use of Wastewater – Piloting the monitoring methodology and initial findings for SDG indicator 6.3.1 By WHO and UN-Habitat on behalf of UN-Water	Leaking latrines and raw wastewater can spread disease and provide a breeding ground for mosquitoes, as well as pollute groundwater and surface water. Learn more about wastewater monitoring and initial status findings here: http://www.unwater.org/publications/progress-on-wastewater-treatment-631.
Progress on Ambient Water Quality – Piloting the monitoring methodology and initial findings for SDG indicator 6.3.2 By UN Environment on behalf of UN-Water	Good ambient water quality ensures the continued availability of important freshwater ecosystem services and does not negatively affect human health. Untreated wastewater from domestic sources, industry and agriculture can be detrimental to ambient water quality. Regular monitoring of freshwaters allows for the timely response to potential sources of pollution and enables stricter enforcement of laws and discharge permits. Learn more about water quality monitoring and initial status findings here: http://www.unwater.org/publications/progress-on-ambient-water-quality-632.
Progress on Water-Use Efficiency – Global baseline for SDG indicator 6.4.1 By FAO on behalf of UN-Water	Freshwater is used by all sectors of society, with agriculture being the biggest user overall. The global indicator on water-use efficiency tracks to what extent a country's economic growth is dependent on the use of water resources, and enables policy- and decision makers to target interventions at sectors with high water use and low levels of improved efficiency over time. Learn more about the baseline situation for SDG indicator 6.4.1 here: http://www.unwater.org/publications/progress-on-water-use-efficiency-641.

Progress on Level of Water Stress – Global baseline for SDG indicator 6.4.2 By FAO on behalf of UN-Water	A high level of water stress can have negative effects on economic development, increasing competition and potential conflict among users. This calls for effective supply and demand management policies. Securing environmental water requirements is essential to maintaining ecosystem health and resilience. Learn more about the baseline situation for SDG indicator 6.4.2 here: http://www.unwater.org/publications/progress-on-level-of-water-stress-642.
Progress on Integrated Water Resources Management – Global baseline for SDG indicator 6.5.1 By UN Environment on behalf of UN-Water	Integrated water resources management (IWRM) is about balancing the water requirements of society, the economy and the environment. The monitoring of 6.5.1 calls for a participatory approach in which representatives from different sectors and regions are brought together to discuss and validate the questionnaire responses, paving the way for coordination and collaboration beyond monitoring. Learn more about the baseline situation for SDG indicator 6.5.1 here: http://www.unwater.org/publications/progress-on-integrated-water-resources-management-651.
Progress on Transboundary Water Cooperation – Global baseline for SDG indicator 6.5.2 By UNECE and UNESCO on behalf of UN-Water	Most of the world's water resources are shared between countries; where the development and management of water resources has an impact across transboundary basins, cooperation is required. Specific agreements or other arrangements between co-riparian countries are a precondition to ensuring sustainable cooperation. SDG indicator 6.5.2 measures cooperation on both transboundary river and lake basins, and transboundary aquifers. Learn more about the baseline situation for SDG indicator 6.5.2 here: http://www.unwater.org/publications/progress-on-transboundary-water-cooperation-652.
Progress on Water-related Ecosystems – Piloting the monitoring methodology and initial findings for SDG indicator 6.6.1 By UN Environment on behalf of UN-Water	Ecosystems replenish and purify water resources and need to be protected to safeguard human and environmental resilience. Ecosystem monitoring, including that of ecosystem health, highlights the need to protect and conserve ecosystems and enables policy- and decision makers to set de facto management objectives. Learn more about ecosystem monitoring and initial status findings here: http://www.unwater.org/publications/progress-on-water-related-ecosystems-661.
UN-Water Global Analysis and Assessment of Sanitation and Drinking-Water (GLAAS) 2017 report – Financing universal water, sanitation and hygiene under the Sustainable Development Goals (including data on SDG indicators 6.a.1 and 6.b.1) By WHO on behalf of UN-Water	Human and financial resources are needed to implement SDG 6, and international cooperation is essential to making it happen. Defining the procedures for local communities to participate in water and sanitation planning, policy, law and management is vital to ensuring that the needs of everyone in the community are met, and to ensuring the long-term sustainability of water and sanitation solutions. Learn more about the monitoring of international cooperation and stakeholder participation here: http://www.unwater.org/publication_categories/glaas/.
SDG 6 Synthesis Report 2018 on Water and Sanitation By UN-Water	This first synthesis report on SDG 6 seeks to inform discussions among Member States during the High-level Political Forum on Sustainable Development in July 2018. It is an in-depth review and includes data on the global baseline status of SDG 6, the current situation and trends at the global and regional levels, and what more needs to be done to achieve this goal by 2030. Read the report here: http://www.unwater.org/publication_categories/sdg-6-synthesis-report-2018-on-water-and-sanitation/.

UN-Water coordinates the efforts of United Nations entities and international organizations working on water and sanitation issues. By doing so, UN-Water seeks to increase the effectiveness of the support provided to Member States in their efforts towards achieving international agreements on water and sanitation. UN-Water publications draw on the experience and expertise of UN-Water's Members and Partners.

PERIODIC REPORTS

Sustainable Development Goal 6 Synthesis Report 2018 on Water and Sanitation

The SDG 6 Synthesis Report 2018 on Water and Sanitation was published in June 2018 ahead of the High-level Political Forum on Sustainable Development, where Member States reviewed SDG 6 in depth. Representing a joint position from the United Nations family, the report offers guidance to understanding global progress on SDG 6 and its interdependencies with other goals and targets. It also provides insight into how countries can plan and act to ensure that no one is left behind when implementing the 2030 Agenda for Sustainable Development.

Sustainable Development Goal 6 Indicator Reports

This series of reports shows the progress towards targets set out in SDG 6 using the SDG global indicators. The reports are based on country data, compiled and verified by the United Nations organizations serving as custodians of each indicator. The reports show progress on drinking water, sanitation and hygiene (WHO/UNICEF Joint Monitoring Programme for Water Supply, Sanitation and Hygiene for targets 6.1 and 6.2), wastewater treatment and ambient water quality (UN Environment, UN-Habitat and WHO for target 6.3), water-use efficiency and level of water stress (FAO for target 6.4), integrated water resources management and transboundary water cooperation (UN Environment, UNECE and UNESCO for target 6.5), ecosystems (UN Environment for target 6.6) and means for implementing SDG 6 (UN-Water Global Analysis and Assessment of Sanitation and Drinking-Water for targets 6.a and 6.b).

World Water Development Report

This annual report, published by UNESCO on behalf of UN-Water, represents the coherent and integrated response of the United Nations system to freshwater-related issues and emerging challenges. The theme of the report is harmonized with the theme of World Water Day (22 March) and changes annually.

Policy and Analytical Briefs

UN-Water's Policy Briefs provide short and informative policy guidance on the most pressing freshwater-related issues, which draw upon the combined expertise of the United Nations system. Analytical Briefs provide an analysis of emerging issues and may serve as a basis for further research, discussion and future policy guidance.

UN-WATER PLANNED PUBLICATIONS 2018

- Update of UN-Water Policy Brief on Water and Climate Change
- UN-Water Policy Brief on the Water Conventions
- UN-Water Analytical Brief on Water Efficiency

More information on UN-Water Reports at www.unwater.org/publications